The CHEESES *of* WISCONSIN

The CHEESES *of* WISCONSIN

A CULINARY TRAVEL GUIDE

JEANETTE HURT

THE COUNTRYMAN PRESS

WOODSTOCK, VERMONT

Published by The Countryman Press, P.O. Box 748, Woodstock, Vermont 05091

Distributed by W. W. Norton & Company, Inc., 500 Fifth Avenue, New York, NY 10110

Printed in the United States of America

10 9 8 7 6 5 4 3 2 1

This book is dedicated to my husband, Kyle Edwards, whose very first job was as a cheese boy at the Highlands Cheese Basket in Racine, Wisconsin.

ACKNOWLEDGMENTS

THIS BOOK COULD NOT HAVE BEEN WRITTEN WITHOUT THE assistance of so many people, and I may be remiss in thanking some of you, for which I apologize in advance. I owe a great deal of gratitude to all of the wonderful folks at the Wisconsin Milk Marketing Board (WMMB) and the Dairy Business Innovation Center (DBIC). Special thanks goes out to Heather Porter Engwall, Marilyn Wilkinson, Megan Bykowski, Patrick Geoghegan, and Mary Litviak from the WMMB, and to Norm Monsen and Jeanne Carpenter from the DBIC. It also would not have been possible if Steve Ehlers and Patty Peterson (and Larry, too), of Larry's Market, had not introduced me to the wonderful world of Wisconsin artisanal cheese so many years ago. Thanks for feeding my addiction. Also, a special thanks goes out to the many people who helped me arrange my trips to visit cheesemakers—Al Chechik, Joan Collins, Jean Freidl, Allyson Gommer, Lisa Marshall, Noreen Rueckert, and Debi Smith. Thanks goes out to my family and friends, especially Tom, Julie, and Karen Hurt; Jeanne and Ed Potter; Craig Edwards and Sally Dowhower; Ellen and Dick Haynes; and Damon Brown; but especially to my wonderful mother, Mary Hurt, who took on the herculean task of indexing this book. Gratitude is also owed to my wonderful editorial team: Kermit Hummel, Kim Grant, Jennifer Thompson, and Sandy Rodgers. Thanks goes out to my Webmaster, Bec Loss Hartel, and thanks to all the chefs, sommeliers, and cheese experts who took the time to answer my many questions, but most of all, heartfelt thanks goes out to the cheesemakers who invited me into their lives and their world. This is for you.

CONTENTS

APPENDICES

INTRODUCTION

"Cheese is milk's leap toward immortality."
—CLIFF FADIMAN

'M NOT A BIG SHOE SHOPPER. CLOTHES DON'T MUCH TEMPT ME, either. And I never shop for antique baubles or collectibles of any sort. But I have been known to drop $100 or more on cheese.

Blame it on my heritage. I'm the granddaughter of a Wisconsin dairy farmer, and my great- great- great-grandparents were the first settlers in Pine Creek, Wisconsin, moving their family's farming operation from Poland to the United States before the Civil War.

I can't quite blame my yearning for cheese on my roots. I am actually an urban girl, having grown up in Chicago and then moving to Milwaukee as an adult. Although I fondly remember eating apple and Muenster cheese sandwiches as a child, my fondness for aged dairy goodness really started when I was in college.

As an exchange student in Madrid I discovered a penchant for Manchego. Then, while traveling with friends, I fell hopelessly, madly in love with Curé Nantais, a rare bloomy rind cheese one only really happens upon while in the Loire Valley. Returning to the States and starting up my career as a writer, I satisfied my cravings with imported Roquefort and Brie, mixing things up with the occasional Parmigiano Reggiano or Gouda.

About 10 years ago, though, my world changed, and I owe it all to my friend and cheese dealer, Steve Ehlers. Steve, who owns Larry's Brown Deer Market, suggested that I might want to try some artisanal cheeses in addition to my regular purchases. After my first questions of what are they and why should I care about something made outside of France, I soon was swooning. Old Chatham's Sheepherding Camembert blew me out of the water—it was fresher and creamier than the imported varieties I was used to. Cowgirl Creamery's stinky cheeses sunk their claws into me. Great Hill's blue made me stray from my beloved Roquefort. I was hooked.

Six years ago, Steve threw my planet into another orbit, and my cheese palate evolved. He introduced me to Mike Gingrich, whose Pleasant Ridge Reserve rocked the cheese world when it took top honors at the 2001 American Cheese Society's competition, in its very first year of production. Then, Sid Cook wooed me with his mastery of mixed milk cheeses. And now I am torn between Bruce Workman's heady Emmentaler and Brenda Jensen's creamy sheep's milk magic.

Savory or sweet, crumbly or creamy, these cheeses made my mouth water, and when they were gone from my cupboard, I would dream about them at night. As a food and wine writer, I knew I was on to something, something big.

In a sense, my cheese palate expanded, and Wisconsin cheesemakers were ready for me. Not that they personally set their aspirations on satisfying my odd, goat's milk cheese craving (though maybe they did—I've never asked them). But statistically speaking, Wisconsin went from making perhaps a couple dozen farmstead and artisanal cheeses in the early 90s, most of them of the cheddar variety, to well over 900 that are produced today.

I like to think that my Grandpa Rudnik would have enjoyed these cheeses. Though he's long since passed, I think he would be proud of them. And I am more than proud to introduce you, dear readers, to one of my life's great passions: Wisconsin's best cheesemakers and their fine, fine creations. I hope you're hungry.

CHAPTER 1

How Wisconsin Has Become the Leader of the

ARTISANAL CHEESE MOVEMENT

THE EARTH DIDN'T EXACTLY QUAKE WHEN MIKE AND CAROL Gingrich and Dan and Jeanne Patenaude won Best of Show for their cheese at the American Cheese Society's 2001 competition. Still, the rumblings in cheese circles were felt the world over.

That they won with their first ever batch of raw, pasture-grazed Pleasant Ridge Reserve was significant enough. But the real significance was in the dawning change of perception in cheese—Wisconsin cheese, that is.

The Dairy State has been synonymous with cheese since 1910, when it edged out New York to become the leading cheese-producing state in the nation. Plenty of people know that Wisconsin produces cheese, good cheese. However, many people only think of commodity cheeses, especially cheddar, when they think of Wisconsin. This view hasn't been helped by the cheddar-esque foam hats that all good Green Bay Packers fans don at nationally televised football games (never mind that the hats themselves are not supposed to represent any particular

Expanse of lovely green pasture

variety of cheese). The state "cheesehead" or "cheddarhead" monikers, bestowed upon us by our neighboring Bears fans to the south, also reinforce this perception. "It's the yellow cheese syndrome," more than one Wisconsin cheese expert has complained to me.

Yes, Wisconsin does make a lot of cheddar, and yes, more than a few big cheese plants make their headquarters in Wisconsin. Yet that's only part of the Wisconsin cheese story, and it's not the facet of the cheese industry that's growing phenomenally in the state. Wisconsin actually makes almost 50 percent of the specialty cheese production in the United States. In 2005, Wisconsin's share of that production was 46.5 percent. Since 1995, specialty cheese production in the Dairy State has more than tripled, from just under 100 million pounds to 387 million pounds in 2007, accounting for 16 percent of the state's total cheese output, and it continues to grow.

Cheese is big business in Wisconsin, since the $21 billion dairy business is the state's largest industry—ahead of tourism, which is $11 billion. In fact, cheese is more important to Wisconsin than potatoes are to Idaho, and than oranges are to Florida. Although these are big, big numbers, the actual cheese producers and dairy farmers are mostly small in size. The average herd of cows in Wisconsin is only 80 head of cattle, making it smaller than Vermont's 100 head and much smaller than California's nearly 800 head.

When it comes to commodity cheese and milk, the biggest plants in the country aren't in Wisconsin at all—they're out West, in California and New Mexico, or down south, in Texas. California eclipsed Wisconsin in overall milk production in 1993, and for the last couple of years it has been predicted that it will eventually make more cheese than Wisconsin does. But the big cheese numbers in California and elsewhere are being fueled mostly by big plants.

Annually, Wisconsin also continues to win more than any other state or country in national cheese competitions. For example, in 2006 alone, Wisconsin took home 56 awards at the World Cheese Championship and 68 at the American Cheese Society Championship, with about two dozen of them first place or best of class. Those were just two competitions in an ordinary year. You see, in Wisconsin, extraordinary cheese is pretty ordinary.

Ordinary in Wisconsin also means extraordinary in the actual kinds of cheese produced. The actual diversity in other cheese states isn't coming close to what Wisconsin does. Wisconsin, in fact, produces more than 1,000 different kinds of dairy products, most of them cheeses. On the record, state agricultural officials say that Wisconsin produces more than 600 different types and varieties of cheese. Off the record, however, they admit that the real number is actually closer to 1,000. "But we can't come right out and say that because our variety used to be much lower even just a decade ago," says one such official. "No one would believe us if we actually told them how many types of cheeses are made here. They would think it's untrue hype."

While it remains less publicized, the truth is that Wisconsin's cheese industry has fundamentally shifted. Today, there are more farmstead and small independent creameries than the state has seen in several years.

To better understand this phenomenon, it helps to know a little bit about Wisconsin's dairy history. Wisconsin was not always so dairy-centric. In fact, from the time of its earliest beginnings as a territory and continuing past the end of the Civil War, wheat was the main crop in Wisconsin. When wheat began to fail because of soil leaching and bugs, some farmers tried hops, which married nicely with the state's breweries, but that crop didn't have economic staying power.

Dairy came into the picture as a viable economic alternative, and gradually, from the 1870s through the turn of the century, farmers shifted from cultivating wheat to nurturing dairy cattle. What followed was a combination of factors that set the stage to build Wisconsin as a dairy state. The Wisconsin Dairymen's Association started up in 1872, and a college of agriculture was established at the University of Wisconsin-Madison in 1889. Around the same time, Swiss immigrants in Green County saw opportunity in switching from wheat to dairy, and they easily implemented their knowledge of cheesemaking.

Giant wheels of "Green County" Swiss age

In its infancy, quality standards had to be set. The simple fact was that Wisconsin needed to make superlative cheese—just in order to be able to compete with New York, the country's first center for dairy. Milk quality became strictly enforced with state-regulated rules, and the Wisconsin Cheese Makers

Association, formed in 1893, laid down the law to make sure no short-cuts were taken in cheesemaking.

From the turn of the century until the 1920s, cheesemaking exploded, and Wisconsin earned its reputation as "America's Dairyland." Adding to this mystique were two innovative cheesemakers who created American originals, cheeses never before tasted. Brick cheese was invented in 1877 by John Jossi, a Swiss-born cheesemaker, and Colby cheese was developed in 1885 by Joseph Steinwand. Cheesemaking grew to an all-time high of 2,807 cheese factories in 1922. It used to be

Bert Paris's "Happy Wisconsin" bovines eat at the feed bunk in colder months when they cannot be rotationally grazed

said that every small town in Wisconsin had a church, a tavern, and a cheese plant. Though these small plants consolidated and closed up through the 1970s, overall cheese production grew, and Wisconsin's reputation as *the* Dairy State became firmly established.

The same strict regulations that helped establish Wisconsin's dairy reputation continue on to this very day. Laws governing cheese production are more stringent in Wisconsin than anywhere else in the nation. In order to sell your cheese to people outside your family, you have to go through a rigorous licensing process. To get your cheese license, you have to take several university-level classes and complete an apprenticeship.

Wisconsin also is the only state that offers a master cheesemaker's certification, which is modeled after the European system of apprenticeship. A cheesemaker can only be certified in two cheeses at any given time. In order to even apply for certification, he or she has to have been making that cheese for at least five years. Then, the cheesemaker enrolls in the master cheesemaking program, which takes an additional three years to complete. During that time, cheesemakers must take several classes, and at the end, their cheeses are judged formally.

Such regimented laws have aided the plethora of cheese, dairy, and agricultural resources in the state. Those same organizations like the Wisconsin Cheese Makers Association, which helped foster the state's dairy industry, are not only around today, they are greatly more numerous, with more than 20 different dairy-related government agencies and private businesses. This combination—of laws and resources—means that Wisconsin sets a standard for the utmost quality in cheesemaking, and that it has the wherewithal and knowledge to not only continue, but to further the tradition of cheesemaking.

This still doesn't quite explain the tremendous rise in artisanal and specialty cheeses that seemingly happened overnight, or rather, occurred in just the last five to seven years in Wisconsin. For many years, the twin pillars of cheesemaking—the strict rules and the dairy agencies—simply aided commodity and small-factory cheesemaking. Not that they weren't good cheeses. The cheeses simply were either not extraordinary, or if they were incredible, they were also incredibly local commodities.

The recent flourishing of artisanal cheeses

Some wheels of Wisconsin's most decorated cheese—Pleasant Ridge Reserve—age

can be explained by three different factors, factors that are all related to the surprising big win of Pleasant Ridge Reserve in 2001.

The first explanation is that most of the original cheesemakers in Wisconsin were artisans themselves. Small, tiny factories run with the help of less than a handful of hands were the base of Wisconsin's cheese industry. As such, several individual cheesemakers never consolidated or closed, and they and their subsequent generations have continued to make small, high quality batches of cheeses. What Pleasant Ridge Reserve's win did, however, was to wake up these cheesemakers to the potential their cheeses had, in both marketing and scope; it opened their eyes to the possibility of growing their customer base beyond the state's borders.

The second reason is the reality that most of the state's cheesemakers, at both small and larger companies, always made specialty cheese. "Twenty or even thirty years ago, we created special cheeses that we aged for several years," says Sid Cook, an award-winning, fourth generation cheesemaker. "But we didn't sell them to the public." The rise in consumer interest in fine cheeses across the country in the 1990s, however, began inspiring state cheesemakers to sell their private stashes—especially to those caseophiles and chefs who combed the countryside, looking for something new or different.

Lastly, the third root goes back to Wisconsin's tradition—its strict rules and its deeply imbedded infrastructure. Wisconsin cows produce good milk, and the state has the knowledge to help existing and budding cheesemakers. That's why, in fact, Mike Gingrich chose Wisconsin as the home base for his cheesemaking. Though he had grown up on a Midwestern dairy, he and Carol, his high school sweetheart, moved to California so he could embark on a professional career path with Xerox Corporation. When he and Carol decided to return to farming, there was no question about where they wanted to graze their cows.

Mike's big win not only woke up the cheese world outside of Wisconsin, causing them to perceive the state's cheese prowess in a new light, but it also jolted the state's dairy community out of its complacency. It made dairy insiders aware of the ability of Wisconsin cheesemakers to produce not only good, standard varieties of cheese, but that they could also make stellar, American originals, cheeses the world has never before tasted.

Now, while there were other cheesemakers who had been making specialty and artisanal cheeses before the Gingriches and the Patenaudes, there hadn't been a cheese to ever before rise to such prominence so quickly. Their daring has not only inspired cheesemakers and dairy farmers within the state to try new endeavors, but it has also attracted other experienced and novel cheesemakers from around the world—cheesemakers who have since moved to Wisconsin to make their cheeses.

In fact, as I write this, dozens of new cheesemakers are working with the state's Dairy Business Innovation Center to come online with their cheeses by 2008. And each one of them has the potential to make the next Pleasant Ridge Reserve.

CHAPTER 2

How to Make Cheese,
WISCONSIN
STYLE

T ALL STARTS WITH THE MILK. MILK MIGHT DO A BODY GOOD, but it also does a cheese good, and any good cheesemaker will tell you that without great milk, you're not going to get great cheese.

Wisconsin happens to offer some of the best geographical and climatological areas on the globe for raising dairy cows. Other states' marketing campaigns might celebrate jubilant bovines, but the truth is, cows prefer weather that's a bit on the cold side, about 50 degrees Fahrenheit, the same temperature as a crisp, cool fall or spring day in Wisconsin. Combined with the state's abundance of natural limestone water and fecund green pastures, these temperatures—especially in autumn—provide some of the most luscious and luxurious milks you could ever savor.

"We are sitting on top of one of the richest cheesemaking regions on the planet," says Patrick Geoghegan, senior vice president of the Wisconsin Milk Marketing Board and president of the Dairy Business Innovation Center.

Wisconsin pours 90 percent of its velvety and delicious milk into cheesemaking. And the state isn't just known for cow's milk, but for goat's and sheep's milk, too. In fact, Wisconsin

Holsteins are the most popular breed of milking cows on the planet, especially in Wisconsin, because they are also the most productive.

produces more goat's milk than any other state.

On farmstead cheesemaking operations, the milk is just pumped or carried by hand in pails from the milking room into either the pasteurizing room or the cheesemaking room, depending on the cheese and the cheesemaker's individual setup. In smaller operations, it's contained in a temperature controlled vat until the cheesemaker has enough milk to make cheese.

For cheesemakers who do not run their own farms, milk comes to their creameries primarily from two different types of farms: those that use rotational grazing techniques and those that use traditional, or silage and hay fed cows. In rotational grazing, the cows are moved into different pastures every 12 hours. "It's like giving them a clean plate," says Bert Paris, a dairy farmer and advocate of rotational grazing who is a partner in Edelweiss Town Hall Creamery. "And if I don't rotate them on time, they'll let me know."

With the more traditional or silage method of farming, the dairy farmers not only take care of their cows, but they also grow the clover, wheat, and other ingredients that go into the cattle feed. Most of these farmers also do not use any bovine growth hormone (rBGH) to increase their production because cheesemakers would refuse to accept their milk. In order to become a milk supplier, the farmers need to sign legal documents certifying that their milk is rBGH-free.

The average farmer in Wisconsin only has a herd of 80 cattle, a size that allows the farmers to know each one of their cows. In turn, the cheesemakers know what each particular farm offers, and some cheesemakers pick milk from specific farms to make specific cheeses. "When I'm making a certain batch of cheese, I specify to my delivery driver which farms he should pick up milk at," says Tony Hook, of Hook Cheese in Mineral Point. "Different milks lend different qualities to each cheese."

Another source for milk is Amish farms. Typically, an Amish farmer will have only 12 or 14 cows, sheep, or goats, and they use very natural, noninvasive methods of farming. Their milk, unlike the milk from regular dairy farms, arrives all in cans. "In the early days, everyone used cans," says Melbourne "Sam" Cook, a retired cheesemaker and father of noted cheesemaker Sid Cook. "The farmers used to haul their milk in the back of pickup trucks. That changed, but the process of cheesemaking, if you discount the modern machinery, is still basically the same."

That process starts as soon as the milk is unloaded at the cheese factory or as soon as it is milked at a farmstead operation. The milk is transferred from either the trucks or the animals to holding tanks. From the holding tanks, it's then transferred to a pasteurizer, if the milk being used for a cheese calls for pasteurization. If it is raw or unpasteurized, then it is pumped directly into heated vats (which is where the pasteurized milk

Diana Murphy feeds her herd of friendly goats

goes after pasteurization), and bacterial cultures are added to start the process. Different cultures produce different cheeses. For example, cheddars typically use a mesophilic culture while most blue cheeses use *Penicillium roqueforti*.

But each cheesemaker has his or her own special formula of cultures. No two cheddars, for example, have the exact same recipe. Many cheesemakers experiment with different cultures and blends of cultures when they are creating new cheeses.

After the cultures work their magic—which usually takes about 45 minutes—then rennet is added. This coagulant originally came from calves' stomachs, but today, most cheeses—excluding some very specific Italian varieties—are made with a microbial form of rennet that has never seen the inside of a baby cow's digestive system. Some cheeses also require different, vegetable-derived coagulants.

Bert Paris and his farm dog check out the fields

The rennet is stirred into the milk, typically with automated paddles that traverse the length of the vat, gracefully swimming to and fro. If the cheese is orange, then annatto, a plant extract, also is added around this time. More and more customers, however, prefer uncolored cheeses.

Then the milk sets, and it looks, feels, and even jiggles like those Jell-O salads your Grandma Marvel used to make for Sunday dinner (minus the mandarin oranges or green olives, however). At this point, the cheese is cut. Cutting the cheese does not cause the emission of gases, but rather, it allows the whey, a watery protein liquid, to separate from the curds. Minus the tuffet, this is exactly what Miss Muffet was chowing down in the nursery rhyme.

Cheesemakers use cheese harps, or metal paddles

strung with linear blades, to cut the cheese. Typically, two cheesemakers will cut the vat together, nimbly dancing their blades lengthwise and then crosswise through the vats. That causes the whey to separate from the curds, and the whey is then drained off, usually through a drain in the bottom of the vat. When the whey is drained, a very small percentage of cream also goes with it. That cream is sold off to the state's butter makers.

The whey is also a sellable product, and it can be added to everything from protein drinks to animal food, providing an additional stream of income for most cheesemakers. Many years past, however, whey was considered a waste by-product. Sometimes, farmers would feed it to their pigs as slop, and sometimes, naughty cheesemakers would dump it in drainage ditches by the roadside. That was back in the years when people still thought smoking was good for you. Today, it's not at all an accepted practice.

From this point on, the cheesemaking process differs from cheese to cheese. Many cheeses, at this juncture, are pumped or poured into molds or shapes, and pressed. Others, like Colby, are washed with water. But for cheddar, this is the time the cheddaring process begins.

The little, inch sized curds begin to stick

Bruce Workman checks to see if his curd is ready

Workman and his assistant drag cheese harps through to separate the curds from the whey

together at this point, and a cheesemaker drains a line down the center of the table. Then the curd mass is cut into large, thick slabs. These slabs are then piled up and turned several times—about four or five times, one turn every 15 minutes. This process—the cheddaring—presses the curds together more tightly, and even more whey drains out. The slabs start out several inches thick, and by the time the cheddaring is accomplished, they look like 1-inch-thick, fluffy yellow (or white) pillows. The slabs are then recut into curds, and salted.

Salt not only gives cheese flavor, but it also preserves the cheese, and it slows down the bacterial cultures. Salt, in cheddar, is added through the dry salt method. "We actually lose about half of our salt because more whey will drain out and take the salt with it," says Kerry Henning, a master cheesemaker and owner of Henning Cheese in Kiel.

Two other methods of salting are used. Swiss cheese, for example, requires brining, and the wheels will soak in brine to absorb the salt—sometimes for several days, if they are big wheels. Other cheeses have the salt applied through dry rubbing.

With cheddar, after the salt is added to the curds, a good percentage of the curds are often just sold as is to lines of customers. Some cheesemakers add dill, garlic, and other seasonings, but curds are equally popular just plain. Fresh, warm curds are a popular snack in Wisconsin. You can always tell if curds are really fresh because they squeak in your mouth. Curd is also popular when it's served breaded, fried, and accompanied with dipping sauces, especially at county fairs and at the Wisconsin State Fair. Curds are so popular that Wisconsin native and Arctic explorer Eric Larsen even took some along with him as a pick-me-up when he and Lonnie Dupre became the first explorers to ever reach the North Pole in the summer.

And unlike regular cow's milk cheeses, cheese curds can be frozen because of their higher water content. In fact, for those who do not live in Wisconsin but wish to experience the squeaking curds, just warm up your curds in the microwave for a few seconds. The heat will give them their squeak back, and you can enjoy an authentic Wisconsin snacking experience no matter where you are. Eric, however, was unable to heat up the curds at the pole, so he and Lonnie just had to eat them cold.

To continue the cheesemaking process, the curds are poured into stainless steel hoops or molds. If the cheese isn't cheddar, then it is brined or dry rubbed with salt after it forms a more solid mass.

From this point on, cheese is aged, and the process of curing and perfecting the cheese begins. Some cheeses are ready almost immediately—fresh chèvre, for example, does not go through an extensive aging process.

But different temperatures and treatments are implemented to create different cheeses. They can be waxed, sprayed, washed, brushed, or salted. Molds can be added to create bloomy or hard rinds. Some cheeses, like blue cheeses, are punched with holes, so that circulating air can encourage the "bluing" of the cheese.

Bruce Workman's assistant cuts the cheese crosswise after cutting it length-wise.

The ripening or affinage of cheese begins. Historically, in France anyway, cheeses were perfected by the affineur, who would tend to the aging cheeses carefully. Here, however, the cheesemakers take on that role. "You have to know which cheeses are going to age well, and you have to be able to imagine how they will taste a year out, two years out, or ten years out," says Tony Hook, who with his wife, Julie, age out their best cheddars from 4 to 12 years.

Most truly great cheeses require aging, and by law, any cheese that is made from unpasteurized or raw milk must be aged for at least 60 days. Many cheesemakers wish this law wasn't so uncompromising, since there are numerous, wonderful European cheeses made from raw milk that aren't aged. And at least one innovative Wisconsin cheesemaker has found a loophole in the law by selling such fresh cheeses as "fish bait."

Lastly, the cheeses are packaged, marketed, and sold, either directly to consumers through the Internet or at farmers' markets. Many great Wisconsin cheesemakers, including the Hooks, sell their cheeses at the Dane County Farmer's Market in Madison, the country's largest farmer's market. In the summer months it is held right in the middle of the capitol, and off-season, it is held inside.

Cheeses are sold to stores and restaurants, either directly or through distributors. Though this is the last step in the cheesemaking process, before the cheese leaves the cheesemaker's hands and ends up in your mouth, it is an important one, and many cheesemakers are actually picky about who they sell their cheeses to. Fine cheesemakers want to ensure that their craftsmanship is handled and nurtured carefully. "I won't sell my cheese to just anyone," says Brenda Jensen, who makes fresh, creamy sheep's milk cheese at her farmstead operation in Westby. "I'm very particular who I sell my cheeses to."

The CHEESEMAKERS

CHAPTER 3

The Cheesemakers of

SOUTHWESTERN

WISCONSIN

Joe Milinovich stands in front of an aging rack of Pleasant Ridge Reserve cheese

UPLANDS CHEESE COMPANY

5023 State Road 23 North
Dodgeville, WI 53533
608-935-5558
www.uplandscheese.com
PLEASANT RIDGE RESERVE

The first year Mike and Carol Gingrich and Dan and Jeanne Patenaude put their cheese on the market, it made quite a splash in the milk pail, earning the championship cheese title at the American Cheese Society's 2001 show. Though these two farm families had only been making cheese for two years, their win wasn't a fluke. They blasted the competition in 2005 when they won Best of Show again, their product becoming only the second cheese in the country to earn top honors twice. In 2003, Pleasant Ridge Reserve also earned more accolades, being named U.S. Champion at the 2003 U.S. Championship cheese contest. Pleasant Ridge Reserve is the only cheese to ever win both national competitions.

"Anyone who knows anything about cheese knows and loves Pleasant Ridge Reserve," says Richard Peterson, maître fromager at Old Hickory, the signature restaurant at Nashville's Gaylord Opryland Resort. "It's one of the truly great American cheeses."

Before it started appearing in gourmet cheese shops and upscale restaurants, Pleasant Ridge Reserve was just an idea of a couple friends. Back in 1994, these two couples decided to embark on a joint endeavor. The Gingriches had been living in California at the time, but they wanted to get back to farming, so they decided to form a partnership with the Pate-naudes. They pooled together their resources to purchase 300 acres in Dodgeville, Wisconsin, with the idea that they would make cheese.

However, they didn't just start mixing curds and whey together. Their cheese plan started with their cows, specially planted pastures, and a rotational grazing system. The pastures are made up of 30 percent clover and different grasses. "It's the highest nutritional content for the cows," says Joe Milinovich, a cheesemaker who works with Mike. Rotational grazing means that the cows are moved to a different pasture throughout the day. That keeps the land healthier, as the cows don't overgraze the fields, but it also keeps the cows and their milk healthier as grass is at its height of nutrition when it reaches between 8 and 12 inches. That means that the milk also has a better, richer flavor. The downfall is that the cows only graze from spring until fall, and the cheese production doesn't even begin until the cows have been grazed on a full grass diet for at least one full week. "We're dedicated to only use the milk when the cows are on full pasture," Joe says.

Despite the seasonal drawback, these two couples knew that they had ready access to superior milk, and they decided that they needed to come up with a cheese worthy of that milk. To do that, they began studying the different cheeses of the world that were made just from grass-fed, pastured cows, and then specially ordered those cheeses, trying to figure out what kind they'd like to make. "After several tast-

Even though it's not finished aging, Pleasant Ridge Reserve cheese still shows off a lovely golden hue.

ings, we decided on a cheese from the French Alps called Beaufort," Mike Gingrich says. "We couldn't exactly replicate the alpine environment, but we decided to try to make that sort of cheese anyway."

Working with the Center for Dairy Research at the University of Wisconsin and the deep archives of the Wisconsin Milk Marketing board, they tried out several different batches of Beaufort, using slightly different procedures. Thirty-two wheels of cheese later, they found their winner.

Although they had their recipe, they still didn't have any place to make their cheese. Bob Wills, owner of the nearby Cedar Grove Cheese creamery, let them use his factory on weekends to make their cheese. The couples also rented refrigerator space at a commercial kitchen to use as an aging room. While they used the same bacteria as is used in the French Beauforts, and aged the cheese in a room that was kept at the same temperature as the French caves, their cheese ended up being something entirely different—an American original. It was from this very first batch of their original cheese that they won Best of Show.

Today, they've grown a bit beyond borrowing the space of others, and they have constructed a small factory of their own at their farm. "You can't make our cheese anywhere else—our soil profile, our cows, and our methods are unique," Joe says. "Still, a lady from France came to visit and told us, 'This is a Beaufort plant.'"

HIDDEN SPRINGS CREAMERY

S1597 Hanson Road

Westby, WI 54667

608-634-2521

www.hiddenspringscreamery.com

DRIFTLESS FRESH SHEEP'S MILK CHEESES

Brenda Jensen stands between her field-plowing draft horses

Brenda Jensen was open to unusual ideas about farming. In fact, she and her husband had been running their hobby farm in Westby, Wisconsin, without any heavy equipment, instead plowing with draft horses. Still, she thought her husband, Dean, was a bit off his rocker when he said he wanted to get into dairy sheep. "People don't milk sheep, and the ones who do are pretty peculiar," Brenda recalls thinking.

But her husband was persistent, and he soon lured her into attending meetings with the Wisconsin Sheep Dairy Cooperative. After a few years of planning, they purchased their first sheep, and soon they began selling their milk to cheese and yogurt companies out of state.

"We just had this wonderful milk, and I thought, 'We can do something with this,'" Jensen says. "I took some artisanal cheese courses, and it just took me. I felt this real connection with the cheese. Then, I thought, 'Maybe I can do this, too.'"

Jensen began apprenticing as a cheesemaker, and she left her executive job in manufacturing in 2006 to pursue cheesemaking. "I felt that if I didn't start it, then I'd never start it," Jensen says. "It was more of a heartfelt decision."

Her decision was welcomed by every local and regional store she approached. "I just had

Brenda Jensen's sheep are protected from predators by a miniature donkey.

to say, 'I have fresh sheep's milk cheese,'" Jensen says. After selling out her first season's cheeses, Jensen and her husband decided to construct a small cheesemaking plant on their farm. The new plant not only gives her more room to focus on her flavors of fresh cheeses, but she also has a cave to experiment with aged versions as well.

Less than a year into her cheesemaking venture, her cheeses took first, second, and fourth in the 2007 U.S. Cheese Championship, and she also won first place and two thirds at the 2007 American Cheese Society competition. "I just entered the competition to learn because I wanted to get back the critiques they do of your cheeses," Jensen says. "When I learned I had won, I thought 'Oh my goodness!' I'm just so grateful. I love the cheese, and I'm just so grateful to have it recognized."

K & K CHEESE/NATURAL VALLEY CHEESES AND PASTURE PRIDE CHEESES

S10 County Highway D
Cashton, WI 54619
608-654-5580
COW, GOAT, AND MIXED MILK CHEESES

Tom Torkelson and Bentley Lein, marketing director, show off wheels of Tom's beautiful cheese

For Tom Torkelson at K & K Cheese, his cheese starts and ends with the milk. Having grown up on a dairy farm, this master cheesemaker knows that all great cheese starts with the milk. His milk, though it comes from 300 cow farms and 15 goat farms, arrives in small amounts in metal buckets, not pump trucks. Each cow and goat is milked by hand, too, since all of his farmers are Amish, and the average size of each farm is about 12 cows or goats. "About 10 percent of our milk is certified organic, but in reality, they're all organic," Tom says. "Their cows and goats are humanely treated, and our whole milk supply is grass fed. You can't get more organic than what they're doing."

Because the Amish milk their animals by hand, the final product arrives with very little agitation, since it is not pumped at all. "That gives the cheese a whole different flavor," Tom says. "We really want to tell the story of where this fantastic milk comes from."

The milk excites Tom as a cheesemaker, and every season brings different nuances to his cheeses. "In the summer, when it's really hot, the cows drink a lot of water, so the milk is lower in fat," Tom says. "In the fall, there's higher levels of fats and proteins."

Just a scant few miles from Tom's plant is one such farm. After you pull into the winding

A few miles down the road from Tom's cheese plant are Amish farms like this one, which supply all the milk for his cheese.

dirt and gravel drive, a clean, red barn awaits. Just across from the barn and adjacent stone and wood milking parlor is a pen where a few horses roam. When you walk into the barn, a few of the cows calmly turn their heads away from their munching to greet visitors. At larger operations, a lot of times cattle are startled by visitors, and there's a sense of nervousness that can be very palpable. Not so at this farm. The cows are only surprised when their pictures are snapped, since they're not used to the electronic flash of a camera.

"This is really a peaceful way of life," Tom says.

It also is a way of life that gives Tom the kind of raw materials he loves to work and experiment with. His experimentation has turned out quite deliciously, as he's earned several national and international awards. He makes semi-soft, washed rind, and even cave-aged cheeses, not to mention a cow's milk version of Juustoleipa, a Scandinavian baked breadlike cheese that's traditionally made with reindeer milk.

One of his latest creations is the Cow Billy, a cow's and goat's milk blend that's hand-washed and aged in a cave. Cow Billy took second place at the 2007 American Cheese Society competition, and Tom's pretty proud of that.

MT. STERLING CHEESE COOPERATIVE

505 Diagonal Street
Mt. Sterling, WI 54645
608-734-3151
www.buygoatcheese.com
GOAT'S MILK CHEDDAR, JACK, AND BUTTER

Tucked between some rolling hills and apple orchards is a tiny cheese plant. Little in size, the Mt. Sterling Cheese Cooperative is mighty in quality, making perhaps the best raw goat's milk cheddar in the country.

Its story starts in 1976 when a handful of goat farmers banded together to form a co-op. In 1983, they purchased their creamery. "When they started making the goat cheese, people only thought of goat cheese as soft chèvre," says Alan Bekkum, cheesemaker and manager.

Friendly goats like these supply milk to Mount Sterling's little plant.

"They were the first ones to do a cheddar, and they had to compete in the marketplace with cow cheddar, and they couldn't get anyone to try this cheese at first."

But the farmers persisted, and they've earned top honors in their categories at the American Cheese Society and the U.S. Championship Cheese competitions. Today, the co-op consists of 25 farms, and 10 employees make, age, package, and then ship the cheese around the country. What's rather remarkable is that the cooperative hasn't been swallowed up by a bigger co-op or company. "If we'd been doing this with cow's milk, we'd be done," Alan says.

Though the raw cheddar is their biggest seller, they also make a variety of flavored jacks and a whey cream butter. "I'm the only licensed butter maker in the U.S. who makes a goat butter," Alan says.

Someday, though, one of his five sons might become the second licensed butter maker who uses goat's milk. In the summer, his wife, Sarah, and his sons—Scott, Mark, Torger, Dustin, and Evan—help out. "I think I might be able to get at least one of them to follow in my footsteps," Alan says. "Right now, though, they want to play in the NBA or major league baseball."

CAPRI CHEESERY

Box 102
Blue River, WI 53518
608-604-2640
www.capricheesery.com
GOAT, MIXED MILK CHEESES

Every Saturday Felix sells his fresh goat's milk cheeses at the Dane County Farmer's Market.

When Felix Thalhammer's son, Leif, was born, he was quite severely allergic to cow's milk. To help his son, Felix began raising goats on his 100-acre farm in Blue River so that his son would always have a supply of fresh, organic milk that he could drink. "It basically saved his life," Felix says.

Not only did the milk from his 10 does save Leif's life, but it also diverted Felix into a new life—that of a cheesemaker. Because his goats were good milkers, Felix and his family had a lot more milk than they could drink. Felix began experimenting with cheesemaking, and soon he had taught himself how to make some pretty good cheese. Some classes at the University of Wisconsin-Madison helped him, but what really inspired him was a trip back home to Switzerland in 1998 (Felix was born in Winterthur, a small town that is northeast of Zurich). There he met with some Swiss cheesemakers and experienced seasonal cheesemaking (when the Swiss take their cows into Alpine pastures) firsthand. Growing up in Europe surrounded by good cheeses, Felix says, helped define his palate as a cheesemaker. "I was able to make my cheese, then taste it and say, 'I think this would be good,'" Felix says.

The first cheese Felix was drawn to making was feta, and he began selling his cheese every Saturday at the Dane County Farmer's Market in the Capitol Square in Madison. His farm became the first organically certified homestead goat dairy in the Midwest.

Today, Felix still has a small herd of goats, but he gets most of his milk from Amish farmers in Sparta, Tomah, and Elroy, making more than a dozen varieties of handcrafted goat's milk and mixed milk cheeses. On most Saturdays, though, you can still find Felix at the farmer's market, and he's usually accompanied by Leif (now 13), and his daughter, Celeste, 5.

Lines often form around Felix's little stand. Felix, wearing his "Dude, where's my cheese?" T-shirt (a black T-shirt he designed personally that some customers special order because it's so funny), hands out samples and helps direct his customers to the cheeses they're seeking. "I had this cheese at this restaurant once," begins one man, and Felix immediately directs him to his St. Pauliner, a washed rind cheese that's made from a mix of goat's milk and cow's milk.

While Felix helps customers, encouraging them to taste his goat's milk cheddar, and his varieties of feta (both French and Greek styles), Celeste stands by his side, tasting the fetas right along with the customers. "We make this cheese," she proudly tells them.

Celeste helps her father make his cheeses. His fetas are brined, of course. The French feta is aged for at least a year, while the Greek feta can be aged for as long as three years.

Felix also has a line of goat's milk Muenster cheeses—his Bear line of cheeses—and some American originals like Govarti, a combination of Gouda and Havarti, as well as the St. Pauliner and St. Felix washed rinds. These washed rinds are aged from two to three years. "The age makes a huge difference in the taste," Felix says.

Bruce Workman's Swiss ages for several months before it is released.

EDELWEISS TOWN HALL CREAMERY

W6117 County C

Monticello, WI 53570

608-938-4094

TRADITIONAL BIG WHEEL SWISS, PASTURE-GRAZED CHEESES

Bruce Workman likes to say he makes Green County Swiss. Back when he started making cheese—some 35 years ago when he was just 17 years old—he helped make Swiss the old-fashioned way: in big, 200-pound wheels.

But through the years, cheesemakers in Green County and everywhere else in the United States all stopped making these behemoth cheeses. When Bruce purchased an old creamery that dated back to the late 1800s, he decided that he was going to make Swiss cheese the way it was meant to be crafted.

However, before he could make his dream cheese, he had to fix up the plant, which had been shuttered for more than two years. "To be honest, it was a dump," Bruce says. "Everyone thought I was crazy. The boiler room had collapsed, the floors had caved in. The only things original were the walls."

Sweat equity helped Bruce turn the plant around. Once it was up and running, he imported a giant copper kettle from a cheesemaking school that had closed down in Ruti, Switzerland. Then, he set about making Emmentaler cheese. To make four 200-pound wheels, it takes 82,000 pounds of milk, and then each wheel has to be aged out for several months. During the aging process, Bruce washes each rind by hand.

As a result of his efforts, his cheese boasts slightly bigger eyes than most other Swiss, since he makes the cheese according to the older standards. In recent years, the eyes have gotten smaller so that it's easier for deli machines to slice them.

To make sure that the cheese tastes right, Bruce only works with a handful of local farmers who have pledged not to use any growth hormones to increase their milk production. One of his partners in this venture is dairy farmer Bert Paris, who not only treats his cattle humanely, but also feeds them using a rotational grazing system, in which each cow gets 1½ acres to herself, and then is moved to another section of pasture every 12 hours. "They want a clean plate," Bert says.

A cleaner plate for cows also means a fresher tasting milk for cheese, and most of Bruce's cheeses are made with this golden-hued milk. Though he only makes a limited amount of pasture-grazed Emmentaler, he specializes in making grazed milk cheddars, Goudas, and jacks. "It's amazing," Bert says. "When we delivered the first load of pasture-grazed milk, Bruce called me over and said, 'Look in the vat.' I looked at the color, and the color of the milk was different because of the grass. I looked at my wife, Trish, and said, 'Wow.' I suspected that the milk would be different, but what a difference."

Since Bruce uses some silage-based milks, the milks are kept completely separate from each other during the cheesemaking processes. In total, Bruce makes about 16 different cheeses, and he tends to focus on the varieties in which he's a bona fide master cheesemaker. "Wisconsin is the only state to have a master cheesemaker program, and to be a master, you

Bruce Workman stands in front of his giant wheels of Swiss. He makes them just the way the Swiss do.

have to have been making the cheese for five years before you enter the program, and then three years after that, and you can only earn masters for two cheeses at a time," Bruce explains.

Right now, Bruce holds five master's certificates, and he's working on two additional master's in Emmentaler and specialty Swiss. When he receives them, he will have more masters licenses than any other cheesemaker in the state.

While Bruce works on his masters, Bert is actively soliciting other dairy farmers to convert to rotational grazing. "The objective is to teach other farmers to use managed, intensive grazing," Bert says. "There's less soil erosion, and the cows are healthier because they get all this exercise. There's even research that suggests that the resulting milk is better for you— some studies show that grass-based milk has higher levels of Omega-3s."

In any case, pasture-grazed milks produce a more honeyed color in cheeses, and the cheeses taste just a little bit richer.

Roth Käse

657 Second Street
Monroe, WI 53566
608-328-2122
www.rothkase.com
Swiss Specialty Cheeses

Horses used to transport Roth Käse's cheese

Roth Käse Swiss is prepared for shipping to the U.S.

Five generations ago, back in 1863, the Roth family began making cheese in Uster, Switzerland, just outside of Zurich. At the turn of the century, Otto Roth, son of founder Oswald Roth, extended the family's cheesemaking enterprises into the world of exports, and he began sending great European cheeses to the United States.

That exporting business laid the foundation for what is today Roth Käse USA. In 1991, Fermo Jaeckle and his cousins Felix and Ulrich Roth decided that the next step would be not to export cheeses, but to make European-styled cheeses in the United States. The cousins chose a region of Green County known as "Little Switzerland" for their venture. Though the area boasts a Heidi festival, they chose it not primarily for the culture, but instead for the milk quality.

"When you have a lot of farmers milking cows, it's only natural that the cheesemakers follow," says Felix. "Switzerland exported a lot of cheesemakers in the 1960s. It's really the quality of the milk."

That quality has been augmented by the array of modern and traditional cheesemaking techniques and recipes that the Roth family brought over from Switzerland. This melding of

Cheese curds are pressed into molds so the whey can drain.

A worker applies a label to Roth Käse's award-winning cheese.

modernism with tradition sets the Roth Käse cheeses apart. The cheeses themselves have earned more than 100 international and national accolades in less than 10 years. "My uncle has a saying, 'Tradition is not the keeping of the ashes; instead, it's the passing of the flame,'" says Kirsten Jaeckle, who is the fifth generation of her family to be involved in cheesemaking. "It kind of sums up what we are trying to do."

That means that the company does some things the old-fashioned way—brining, washing, or waxing some cheeses by hand. Other cheeses are washed by "Sam," a state-of-the-art affinage machine from Europe. Roth Käse also offers a cooperative apprenticeship program in which Swiss and American cheesemakers train in each other's countries, learning each other's methodology.

Roth Käse makes about 75 different cheeses, and one of their latest ventures is a professional kitchen in which visiting chefs can try out their cheeses. The kitchen might also be opened to the public for culinary demonstrations. "If we host any special events here, we would not charge people," Kirsten says. "Our focus has always been on education."

CHALET CHEESE COOPERATIVE

N4858 County Highway N
Monroe, WI 53566
608-325-4343

LIMBURGER AND SWISS CHEESES

Myron Olson shows off a wedge of his award-winning Baby Swiss

Myron Olson grew up on a dairy farm, but he hated cheese. In fact, he was probably the only dairy farming kid in the entire Dairy State who detested cheese. Which is why it is all the more surprising that today, not only does Myron love cheese in all of its varieties, but he is the only master cheesemaker in the country to hold a special Limburger license. That's right, Myron makes the state's number one "stinky" cheese, and he loves every bit of it.

"I was 18 before I ever tasted cheese," Myron says. As a child, Myron would help his father feed a mix of whey and oats to the hogs, and his dad would squeeze fresh rennet from a calf's stomach into the mix. The aroma was similar to cheese, and that completely soured Myron on cheese. If his mother served a platter of cheese and sausage, he'd make sure only to nibble on sausage that hadn't touched any of that vile dairy stuff.

While in high school, though, Myron got a job at a local cheese factory so that he could save some money for college. There, he'd watch his coworkers eat a smidgen of cheese here, a taste of cheese there, and curiosity got the better of him. He tentatively tried a fresh cheese curd . . . soon he was eating cheese and liking it.

In 1971, Myron received his cheesemaker's license, and in 1972, he received a special license to make Limburger. "My license number was 37, and there were only a handful of licenses issued after that," Myron says. "In the 1950s and 60s, there used to be a lot of Swiss plants; in the off season, when they couldn't make a full wheel of Swiss, they would turn to making Limburger, and there was a glut of Limburger in the market, so the government said if you're going to make Limburger, you need a special license."

Not only did Myron receive his license, but he and his new wife moved into the apartment above the cheese plant, of which he eventually became manager. Myron worked while he attended college to receive his bachelor's degree in agricultural economics. Today, Myron works at that same small plant—the Chalet Cheese Cooperative, a farmer's cooperative that started in 1885. It is the only cheese factory in the country that still makes Limburger.

"There's a difference between American Limburger and the Limburger made in Germany or Switzerland," Myron says. "European Limburger smells like sweat socks or a smelly gym bag. Ours is more of an earthy or barny aroma. It's actually not as strong as a lot of the specialty cheeses, like Taleggio for example."

Because of the recent interest in specialty cheeses, Myron worked with the Dairy Research Center to develop some different washed rind cheeses. Although they tasted great, Myron decided not to commit production to them. "I'll let the other guys do that," Myron says. "As for me, I'm going to stick with Limburger."

MONTCHEVRÉ-BETIN

336 Penn Street
Belmont, WI 53510
608-762-5878
www.montchevre.com
GOAT CHEESE

Jean Rossard learned how to make goat's milk cheese in France.

People think of the Wisconsin dairy industry, and they think of cows. But Wisconsin dairy isn't all bovine-related: It also includes goats and sheep in its menagerie. Actually, Wisconsin has more dairy goats, and the biggest production of goat milk, than any other state. Much of that milk is transformed into the fresh and aged goat cheeses at Montchevré-Betin.

Compared to most of the small, artisanal plants, which employ anywhere from 2 to 30 employees, Montchevré is quite a bit larger, with 120 workers who transform a million pounds of milk into cheese every week. But this medium-sized plant isn't a processed cheese facility; instead, it is a specialty plant, and its roots (and technology) lie not in Wisconsin, but in French soil.

Michel Betin and Jean Paul Brassier looked at the American market and decided it might be a good idea to have a foothold in the United States, rather than just to export cheeses here. In 1989, they picked an old Wisconsin cheddar plant that had been shuttered for a decade. After starting up the plant, Jean Paul was killed by a drunk driver when he was in California attending a cheese show.

His son Arnaud took over in his stead, and today, Montchevré is run by Arnaud and his partner, Jean Rossard, a French master cheesemaker. "My dad used to make cheese," Jean

says. "To make cheese, you have to have the feeling and the knowledge, and although I am no longer making cheese by hand like when I started, my experience still helps me today."

Jean and his crew make mostly fresh chèvre, but they also make aged crottins and aged bloomy rinds as well. "Cheese is a life product," Jean says.

Wheels of bloomy-rinded goat's milk cheese are aged in a temperature- and humidity-controlled room.

BRUNKOW CHEESE

17975 County Highway F
Darlington, WI 53530
800-338-3773
CHEDDAR AND AMERICAN ORIGINALS

Joe Burns shows off some of the bandage-wrapped, English-style cheeses

When the Brunkow Cheese plant opened in 1899, it was just one of the many little cheese factories that dotted the Wisconsin countryside. It was started by a group of farmers who had formed a co-op to make it easier on them and their horses, who delivered the cans to plants farther away. In 1929, the cooperative sold the plant to the Geissbuhler family, and today it is run by third-generation cheesemaker Karl Geissbuhler and his partner Greg Schulte.

Like many small cheese plants, Brunkow's basic output included cheddars, jacks, and Swiss varieties, but in the late 1990s they wanted to do something a bit different. Enter Joe Burns, a Chicago wine expert and all around foodie, who began working with Brunkow just as a volunteer to get their fine, rBGH-free cheeses into some of the Chicago farmer's markets.

Joe eventually came on board full-time, and in 2005, he, Karl, and Greg began working on a line of artisanal cheeses inspired by the English countryside. These naturally aged cheeses—including the earthy Little Darling, the unpasteurized Avondale Truckle, and the bandage-wrapped Argylshire—offer them a chance to flex their creative muscles. "We made Little Darling just by chance when we were experimenting," Burns explains. "Because we're

Each one of these wheels is hand-turned during the aging process.

so small, we can experiment. Then, we take the resulting cheeses to the farmer's markets where we can get direct feedback from our customers."

The experimental cheeses are made in a smaller, stainless steel vat that's less than half the size of their normal vats. Then the cheeses are aged in an almost-matching-sized cellar room, which is about the size of a large walk-in closet.

During the summer months Joe puts on a lot of miles, traveling back and forth from Chicago and Madison to the Lafayette plant. One of the biggest draws at the farmer's market is Brunkow's Brun-uusto, a cow's milk version of Scandinavian baked cheese. The cheese, which has a sweet, slightly browned crust, is baked in a small oven at the plant, and it's served hot. At the farmer's markets, Joe heats it up over an open flame, and customers are usually drawn to the toasty cheese. "No one walks by without stopping to get a look at this cheese that caramelizes without melting," Joe says.

HOOK'S CHEESE COMPANY

320 Commerce Street
Mineral Point, WI 53565
608 987-3759

BIG BLUES, GREAT CHEDDARS, AND AWARD-WINNING COLBY

Tony Hook began making cheese 38 years ago, and his wife, Julie, joined him 30 years ago. In 1976, they purchased their first factory, and they raised their children in an apartment above the cheese plant. In 1987, they moved their operations into a plant in Mineral Point that was originally a livery stable.

When they started their cheesemaking ventures, they took standard Wisconsin cheeses

The Dane County Farmer's Market takes over the Capitol Square in Madison every Saturday during the summer.

and brought them up to new levels. In fact, in 1982 Julie became the first woman ever to win the coveted Best of Show from the American Cheese Society for her Colby.

But the longer they made cheese, the more this couple wanted to experiment. They decided to venture into the world of blues in 1997. "They developed faster than we expected," Tony says.

The Hooks make four distinct blue cheeses, which have become nearly as popular as their aged and flavorful cheddars, but the process was wearing on them. "We were doing about 1.5 million pounds a year, and we were running ourselves ragged," Tony says.

So in 2001 they sold off their milk route, but they retained the right to purchase milk from 12 farms. Today, they've scaled down production to a more manageable 50,000 to 100,000 pounds of cheese a year. Depending on the cheese they're making in any given week, Tony will call and arrange to have specific milk from specific farms delivered to meet the exact needs of their cheese. "I used to pick up the milk myself," Tony says. "I knew the quality of my milk, and that's where it's got to start."

That allows Julie and Tony the freedom to try out new cheeses, to invent things like Sweet Constantine—an American original that's similar to a Parmesan, except that it's made with whole milk. Though they distribute cheeses across the country, they sell much of their handwork directly to consumers at the Dane County Farmer's Market in Madison, of which Tony is the president. "It's a good venue for our customers, and we really enjoy it," Tony says.

Some customers, though, like to travel to their Mineral Point plant. If you happen to be traveling through on a Thursday or a Friday, it's a good time to stop by, because those are the days that they're making cheese. Just knock on the unmarked door in the front; they'll answer, and you'll get to see them cutting and stirring their precious gems by hand.

MONTFORTE-WISCONSIN FARMER'S UNION SPECIALTY CHEESE CO.

303 E. Highway 18
Montfort, WI 53569
608-943-6771
MONTFORTE BLUES

Many tourists are lured into the factory store by the promise of fresh cheese curds, which are so fresh they squeak in your mouth.

Sometimes practical business decisions lead to delicious results. The Wisconsin Farmer's Union (WFU) had some extra cash on hand, and they decided they wanted to invest it in a cheese plant. They learned that Winona Foods, a giant food corporation out of Green Bay, needed a more reliable source of blue cheese for their salad dressings. So in 2002, the WFU purchased an old creamery in Montfort.

There, in Montfort, a team of just 24 employees began making just two blue cheeses—Gorgonzola and Montforte Blue—and just about all of their cheeses went to Winona Foods. But since it was a cheese plant, and en route to the Mississippi River, lots of tourists started dropping in to buy cheese, and in 2006, the cheesemakers entered their cheeses into a few contests to see what would happen. The Gorgonzola was crowned best Gorgonzola in the world at the 2006 World Cheese Championship, and the Montforte Blue garnered first in its class at the 2006 American Cheese Society competition. "We really have attracted a lot of attention, and we've gotten new customers as a result," says Penny Heisz, office manager and dairy farmer who supplies some of the rBGH-free milk to the plant. "We're really young, and it's kind of a feather in our cap to have won them."

All of the milk comes from farms like Penny's, farms that are within a 25-mile radius of Montfort. Though the farmer's cooperative has no plans to expand their two-cheese lineup, their little retail store offers products from other Wisconsin artisans, and Penny always encourages visitors to stop next door at the popcorn store. Like Montfort's milk, the popcorn is all made with corn grown on nearby farms.

CHAPTER 4

The Cheesemakers of
SOUTH CENTRAL
WISCONSIN

Cedar Grove's traditional-looking sign belies its innovative cheesemaking process.

CEDAR GROVE CHEESE/ WISCONSIN SHEEP DAIRY COOPERATIVE

E5904 Mill Road

Plain, WI 53577

800-200-6020

www.cedargrovecheese.com

COW'S MILK AND SHEEP'S MILK CHEESES

Sustainability takes on a new meaning at the cheese-making operations of Cedar Grove Cheese. This little, family-owned cheese plant can trace its roots back to 1878, but its philosophy is anything but old-fashioned.

"Businesses take on their owner's personality," says Bob Wills, who with his wife, Beth Nachreiner, purchased the company from Beth's parents in 1989. "I figure, it took us about seven years. I always had this interest in environmental issues."

That interest surfaced first in 1993, when Bob became the first cheesemaker in the country to declare that his cheese was rBGH (recombinant bovine growth hormone)-free. In fact, all of their grass-based cheeses are organic. "I keep trying to figure out what is the next step in having the most benign influence on the environment as possible," Wills says.

For Bob and his wife, the next step came just a decade later when they became the first (and still the only) creamery to have a Living Machine installed to treat the wastewater generated by cheese production. The machine, which is really a system of 10 tanks, purifies the water naturally using tropical plants, microbes, snails, and tiny leechlike creatures. These living organisms treat the 6,000 to 7,000 gallons of wastewater that's produced every day, and after the Living Machine accomplishes its task, the water flows into a lagoon and then is released into Honey Creek, which empties into the Wisconsin River Basin.

Prior to the Living Machine's installation, wastewater was collected and sprayed directly onto nearby farm fields at the cost of three cents per gallon just for labor alone; today, the Living Machine does the same work—without any cost to the environment and for only a half cent per gallon. "The fundamental message of the Living Machine is that if you can make waste visible, people behave differently," Bob says. "People can walk up and see the plants growing and look in the microscope. A lot less water is being used because it's a part of people's consciousness. It changes their behavior, and that is a lesson that has a little broader impact that just what we're doing."

Numerous school groups visit the Living Machine, as do representatives of other cheese factories and small industries, and though there have been a lot of groups who have expressed interest in developing a similar wastewater treatment system, not one of the visitors has actually gone the next step and implemented such a system.

The Living Machine complements the organic array of cheeses that Bob and his staff make, including flavored cheddars and Monterey Jacks, as well as Faarko, a Havarti-like cheese that's made of a blend of sheep's and cow's milks.

Cedar Grove also works with the Wisconsin Sheep Dairy Cooperative to make their aged sheep's milk cheeses. "We were looking for a place to make our cheese, and they have a very good reputation, so we knew they would be able to make a quality product," says Yves Berger, president of the co-op, which is actually based farther north in Wisconsin.

The co-op is made up of 13 farmers in Wisconsin, along with 2 farmers in Minnesota, 1 farmer in Iowa, and 1 farmer in Nebraska. Only the milk from Wisconsin is trekked to Cedar Grove. The group also sells its milk to a few other cheesemakers who make sheep or mixed milk cheeses, and all of its members must produce only Grade A milk. "That's one way of keeping the standards up," Yves explains. "The dairy sheep industry is still rather small, compared to cows or even goats. But sheep milk has twice as much solids, so your yield of cheese will be twice as much. Sheep's milk cheese has a different taste and texture, but I don't want to say that it's a better cheese, as I also love cheese made from cow's milk."

CARR VALLEY CHEESE

S3797 County Trunk Highway G

La Valle, WI 53941

608-986-2781

www.carrvalleycheese.com

COW, GOAT, SHEEP, AND MIXED MILK CHEESES

*Y*ou can't talk about artisanal cheese in Wisconsin without talking about fourth generation cheesemaker Sid Cook. As one of the most innovative and prolific cheesemakers in the country, if not the world, Sid typically cleans up the prizes at national and international cheesemaking competitions, having won more than 150 such awards.

Sid comes from a legacy of Wisconsin cheesemakers. His great-uncle, Ed Lepley, started making cheese when he was 14 years old, and that was in the year 1883. Carr Valley Cheese company was started up in 1902, and like many small creameries, it made the basic lineup of Wisconsin cheeses—cheddars, Colbys, bricks, and maybe some Monterey Jacks. Though Carr Valley still makes a mean aged cheddar and a smoking smoked applewood cheddar, Sid's taken to explore some more unusual avenues of cheesemaking. In the late 1990s, Sid began experimenting with blended milks. "I took a class on Spanish cheeses, and they were all about mixed milk cheeses," Sid says. "I had known of the existence of mixed milk cheeses, but no one in America was doing them."

Sid's first blend of cow's, sheep's, and goat's milk—a ménage—was released to consumers in 1999. "As the cheese aged out, it had more and more character and a personality of its own," Sid says. "As it reached about a year, it started to develop some interesting complexities where you could taste all three milks. The front side is where you could taste the sheep, with an almost sweet, tart flavor, and it was the cow milk that carried it back onto the palate, and the finish is where you could really taste the goat milk."

Experimentation continued—add a schmere here, add a little smoked applewood there, throw in some olive oil for marinating, and even line some with vegetable ash. "The combinations are pretty endless," Sid says.

Sid's creativity was rewarded in 2004 when his aged Gran Canaria, a blend of three milks aged in olive oil, took the Best of Show honors at the American Cheese Society competition. It was the very first time a mixed milk cheese had won top honors in the contest.

Today, Sid makes about 20 different American originals in a lineup of about 60 different cheeses. Not only do consumers from around the country enjoy them, but chefs also cook with them. Because so many chefs use his cheese, Sid decided to open up a cooking school inside his retail outlet in LaValle. Inconspicuously tucked into a strip mall, in the shadow of a Pizza Hut, the school draws in chefs from across the country. Classes are held about once every two weeks in the pristine and elegant kitchen, and they tend to book up fast. The classes run the gamut from grilling the perfect burger to making African stew. "It's just been a lot of fun," Sid says. Just like his cheeses.

Diana Murphy shows off some of her fresh goat's milk cheese at her farm

DREAMFARM

8877 Tablebluff Road
Cross Plains, WI 53528
608-767-3442
www.dreamfarm.biz
FRESH GOAT CHEESE

The computerization of graphic arts and a few pet goats convinced Diana Murphy to leave her commercial art career for her true calling as a cheesemaker. Though Diana grew up on a dairy farm, she had never considered cheesemaking, and in fact, serendipity played a big role. "I like working with my hands and seeing things physically change," Diana says. "Right around the same time as the commercial art world was changing over to computers from hand illustrations, we had moved back to a rural area to grow our family."

Diana and her husband, Jim, bought some chickens and a few goats, and gradually their flocks expanded. After experimenting with some of the extra milk she had, Diana brought some of her cheeses to the local Vernon Valley Community Farm, a small produce co-op that was delivering her eggs to their customers. "They liked my cheeses, and they asked if I'd like to start selling them," Diana says.

In order to commercially make and then sell her cheeses, Diana needed to get her cheese and milk house licenses, so she began taking classes at the University of Wisconsin. Then she did an apprenticeship at Cedar Grove Cheese, under the tutelage of master cheesemaker Robert Wills. Finally, she was ready to make cheese, but she didn't have the proper equipment to make large enough batches to sell. Diana approached Anne Topham of Fantôme Farm, and Anne agreed to let her use her equipment if Diana helped her with her cheeses. Diana agreed, and she made her first batches to sell in 2004. The next year, she was able to set up operations on her little farm. Her organic farm remains small, and though she'd like to grow her herd a bit, she really doesn't want it to get much larger than it is right now; her goats number 18, plus 5 young kids. Her flock of chickens numbers about 400 during the height of the summer season, and she and her family hand-pick, hand-wash, and then label the eggs daily. Each dozen includes two brown eggs and a blue one. Diana also raises a small flock—six ewes and one ram—of Jacob sheep, a primitive breed prized for their wool.

Two of her four daughters, who are not yet away at college, help Diana with the farm chores. "They take turns working with the young stock, and I'll do the milking," Diana says. "They're an important part of the farm, and when they're here, they help out."

As soon as Diana walks into the goat barn, more than 20 pairs of eyes are immediately on her. When she moves closer to their pens they clamor for her loving attention, crowding near her gentle hands, eager for scratches and pats. They're also quite eager to meet any visitors she brings with her, and after they've properly greeted her, the herd clusters around the newcomers, leaving little goat kisses and nibbles on their fingers. "That's why I like goats—they're so interactive," Diana says, removing a plastic bag that one of her ladies pickpocketed from a guest. "Goats are not little cows, and you can't treat them like that."

Diana Murphy milks her goats and makes her cheese right on her farm.

An expert on the art of fresh goat cheese, Diana is working on adding aged cheeses to her repertoire, experimenting with Goudas and other artisanals that she hopes to make available to her customers at the co-op and at the West Side Community Market in Madison. Most recently, Diana took first place in goat's milk fetas at the 2007 American Cheese Society competition. "I'm really a very young cheesemaker," Diana says. "I still feel that I am learning my craft, especially in the art of aged cheeses. I don't deviate from my established recipes yet."

Right now, though, her customers, some from as far away as California, clamor for her fresh milk cheeses. Her male customers tend to go for her garlic dill, while female customers turn toward her herbs de Provence. "I like that I can go full circle," Diana says. "I can milk my goats, see the milk, produce the cheese, give it to my customers, and then get my customers' responses back."

CRAVE BROTHERS FARMSTEAD CHEESE

W11555 Torpy Road

Waterloo, WI 53594

920-478-4887

www.cravecheese.com

*LES FRÈRES AND FRESH MOZZARELLA
AND MASCARPONE*

Though George Crave is the cheesemaker in his family, he's still a dairyman at heart.

The Crave Brothers knew what they were getting into when they decided to start their own dairy farm. In fact, any romantic notions they might have had about agriculture left them when their father left farming in the early 1970s to get a job in town because of economic hardships. Still, the four of them—Charles, George, Thomas, and Mark—loved cows, and dairy farming was in their blood.

So they decided to give it a go, and they started with a 30-cow herd in 1978. After a few years of renting land, they purchased their own farm just northeast of Madison in the little town of Waterloo, where they not only milked their cows, but also grew their own crops to feed their herd of Holsteins. In 2000, they decided to take their farming to the next level and become cheesemakers.

"We knew we had great milk—it's sweet, fresh cream, and it's unique to us," says George, who became their cheesemaker. "But when we decided to cross over and become cheesemakers, it was a whole different world. We were really starting from scratch."

Even though their milk had been used by other cheesemakers for decades, George still had to go through the rigorous training required by the state, and he became an apprentice cheesemaker. He and his brothers also had to decide how they would set up their cheesemaking facility. Several well-meaning "experts" suggested that they build their plant away from their farm, but that advice went against their better instincts. It was also contrary to their desire to see the process go full circle, from crops to cheese, and it didn't fit into their vision of a farmstead cheesemaking operation, one that would go with their strength as farmers. "You have to have a darn good farm, because a cheesemaking operation doesn't run itself," George says. "We decided to build our plant right across the street from our barn."

The first cheese they decided to make was fresh mozzarella, a natural choice given the freshness and sweetness of their milk. The fresh factor also helped them decide on mascarpone and rope cheese. Still, though, they wanted to have their own, signature cheese; a cheese that would tell their story, an original that they could be proud of.

George and his wife, Debbie, traveled to France, where they not only explored the Crave family's French heritage (they're also Irish), but they also really explored the cheeses. In particular, they zeroed in on washed rind cheeses.

After experimenting with different cultures and methods, they settled on the right recipe, and Les Frères was born. "Our first batches were a bit stronger, and we aged them a bit longer," George says.

Les Frères is aged in a special temperature and humidity controlled room, in very small batches. The aging room is adjacent to a new tasting room that they recently completed. The elegant room boasts a state-of-the art kitchen, along with beautiful cherry tables and chairs. The room is open to the public for special events only. "We're not really set up for tours," George says. "In the future, though, that might be something we will do. But right now, our focus is on the cheese and on pampering our cows."

Although all of their cheeses have won awards in national and international cheese competitions, Les Frères is the one they hang their hat on. "We get e-mails from fans around the country, people saying, 'I can't believe this type of cheese is being made in Wisconsin,'" George says. "We're pretty proud of it."

They also listened to their fans seriously, coming up with a smaller version called Le Petit Frere. On the wooden box is a great sketch of Mark, about age 13, with his award-winning show calf, Bubba. "Finally, I'm getting my moment in the sun," says Mark. "Being the youngest, not only of the brothers but of our family of seven, it was about time."

FANTÔME FARM

Route 1
Ridgeway, WI 53582
608-924-1266
www.fantomefarm.com
FRESH AND AGED GOAT CHEESES

A sabbatical in the country and a goat named Angie lured Anne Topham from her academic pursuits and into the realm of cheesemaking. Anne and her partner, Judy Borree, had taken a year off to work on her father's Iowa farm. During that time, he suggested that they get a goat. "He said, 'You can get a goat for money, marbles, or chalk,'" Judy recalls.

An advertisement in the local shopper caught their attention, but when they arrived to look at the goat, the farmer didn't want to sell the goat—he wanted to sell the goat's kid and the goat's grandmother. Anne and Judy left the farm without a goat, but a couple of days later the farmer decided to part with Angelica and her kid. So they loaded up the not-so-angelic goat and Gilda the kid in their pickup truck, and off they went.

That's when things got interesting, because neither Anne nor Judy realized what a good milker Angie would turn out to be. They had so much milk that Anne started making yogurt, but they still had too much milk on their hands. "And neither Judy nor I are big milk drinkers," Anne says.

After a friend returned from France with some bloomy rind goat cheese, Anne was inspired to try her hand at cheesemaking. Like any good academic, Anne headed straight to the library for answers. But this was the early 1980s, and there really wasn't much precedent or research available on farmstead cheesemaking, let alone farmstead goat cheesemaking. An old copy of *Country Woman,* however, had a basic cheese recipe, and that was enough for Anne to get started.

Around the same time that Anne began exploring the art of cheesemaking, their year's sabbatical was almost up. They decided to return to Madison, and Judy returned to academia full-time; but Anne decided to abandon her pursuit of her PhD, and instead, she followed her dream of cheesemaking. The two purchased a farm just north of Mount Horeb, where Judy completely renovated the barn (using wood from an old barn in Iowa) and built a milking room for Anne. "She built it with a hammer and a book," Anne says.

Along the way, Anne discovered how to make fresh goat cheeses. They weren't the bloomy rind variety she dreamed of making, but they were unlike anything else on the market. About that time, a friend clipped an article from the *San Francisco Examiner* about Laura Chenel. "I started trying to call her," Anne says. "I finally reached her, and I explained that I didn't want her recipes—I was already making goat cheese—but I really just wanted to see how she was set up. I needed a visual because here, there were only these very large cheese plants, and none of their operations would be appropriate for me."

Chenel consented, and Anne visited her California cheese plant. She also continued in her quest for knowledge, stumbling upon a French book entitled *The Fabrication of Farmstead Cheeses in France*. Not only was there not an English translation, but there were only two copies of the book in the entire country. Still, Anne's French friend had her mother purchase a copy in Paris and ship it over. Armed with a technical French dictionary, Anne learned the art of farmstead cheesemaking.

Anne also took the necessary classes to become a licensed Wisconsin cheesemaker, receiving her license in 1984. Not only did hers become the first new cheese plant to be licensed in the state in more than 20 years, but she also became Wisconsin's first farmstead goat cheesemaker, and one of the very first farmstead goat cheesemakers in the United States.

Anne and Judy began introducing goat cheese to consumers at the Dane County Farmer's Market in Madison's Capitol Square. Today, they still sell their fresh goat cheeses there, but Anne now also sells her beautiful, bloomy-rinded Fleurie Noir, too. "Cheesemaking is just endlessly fascinating to me," Anne says. "The milk changes throughout the year, and I never make the exact same cheese every week."

In 2005, Anne's cheese received a great honor—it was served at the Thanksgiving dinner, cooked by Chef Tory Miller and the able staff of Madison's L'Etoile, at the James Beard House.

CHAPTER 5

The Cheesemakers of
EASTERN AND NORTHWESTERN WISCONSIN

BASS LAKE CHEESE FACTORY

598 Valley View Trail

Somerset, WI 54025

800-368-2437

www.blcheese.com

COW'S MILK, GOAT'S MILK, AND SHEEP'S MILK SPECIALTY CHEESES

Walking into Bass Lake Cheese Factory is a little bit like stepping back into time. Not only does this little cheese plant in northwest Wisconsin have a lot of history itself, dating back to 1918, but master cheesemaker and owner Scott Erickson's big hobby is collecting antique dairy and farm equipment and accoutrements. Everything from old ice cream advertisements and promotional plastic sippy cow cups (including an exact replica of what this author had as a young girl), to cheese boards and milk thermometers, can be found in the nooks and crannies of this Somerset creamery. Although there are many striking and eye-catching antiques, probably the focal point of Scott's collection is his assortment of antique cream separators, which he sometimes uses for demonstrations for school groups who visit. "The kids look at it like it's unbelievable," Scott says.

What is also almost unbelievable is the diversity of cheeses that Scott handcrafts. With a very small staff, Scott and his wife, Julie, are able to make and market 52 different varieties of cheese. Not only that, but he uses the milk from cows, goats, and sheep to make his cheeses. Scott makes fresh chèvre and aged cheddar, but he also creates some American originals like Canasta Pardo, a creamy sheep's milk cheese that is formed in a basket and hand-painted with cinnamon.

Scott and Julie's journey at Bass Lake began in 1984 when Scott started working at the creamery. "Back then, when I started, it was mostly cheddar, Colby, and co-jack," Scott says. Then the plant was purchased by Olfisco, a company that imported a lot of cheese but wanted to diversify into making more exotic flavors at home. Scott began working with other milks and recipes, and in 1988, his cheese became the first non–cow's milk cheese to win at the Minnesota State Fair.

Around the same time, they also began working with the University of Minnesota on a pilot program of milking sheep, but then the university began selling its sheep's milk cheeses at cow's milk cheese prices, so the company had to shelve the idea of making sheep's milk cheese. Then Olfisco decided to get out of the specialty cheese business,

Bass Lake Cheese Factory hosts wine and cheese tastings every Saturday.

and that's when Scott and Julie stepped in to purchase the historic cheese company. "That first year was a struggle," Scott says.

"But we did it, and we did it all by ourselves," Julie adds.

Purchasing the company allowed Scott to focus on his true love of creating specialty cheeses. Along the way of studying and researching cheeses, Scott received his certification as a master cheesemaker. Not only that, but he also received five different master's certifications, making him (as of 2007) tied with Bruce Workman for having the most master's certifications. "Studying for my master's certifications really allowed me to explore European-styled cheeses," Scott says.

And Scott was finally able to incorporate sheep's milk cheeses into his offerings. Scott has received numerous awards for his cheeses, and he's even traveled abroad to places like Macedonia and Romania to teach new cheesemakers how to make cheese. "I had one cheese

BASS LAKE CHEESE FACTORY, INC.

Besides Scott Erickson's array of artisanal cheeses, the Bass Lake factory store also offers a great selection of wine and Wisconsin products.

judge tell me that he could always tell which cheese I had made just by its taste," Scott says. "To me, that's really one of the highest compliments you could give me."

Julie and Scott's sons, Nick and Josh, have worked with them, and in 1999, when Nick was 15, he became the youngest licensed cheesemaker in the country. The local newspaper did a story about him, which the Associated Press picked up, and then *Good Morning America* flew out to do a story about him, as well. Nick no longer makes cheese, but they still get media attention—especially during football season, because they make green and gold cheese curds, which Packers fans can't eat enough of.

The Packers curds are one of Scott's smaller cheese experiments. His preference, though, is to experiment with old cheese recipes dating back to the early 1900s and the founding of the cheese plant. "These are cheeses you don't see around anymore," Scott says, removing a file from his desk that opens to reveal a Roquefort recipe dating back to 1936. The recipe is typed on fragile, cellophane paper, and handwritten notes are etched on the side, showing what the cheesemaker had tried. "You could spend days going through these files."

BelGioioso Cheese

5810 County Road NN
Denmark, WI 54208
920-863-2123
www.belgioioso.com
Italian Specialty Cheeses

BelGioioso Cheese Company isn't a tiny little artisanal factory, but it makes exquisite cheese, and it played a pivotal role in developing specialty cheese in the state. Indeed, company founder Errico Auricchio is often looked upon as the father of specialty cheese in Wisconsin.

His great-grandfather first got into the cheese business in Naples in 1877. A fourth-generation cheesemaker who grew up near Milan, Errico immigrated to Wisconsin in 1979 with the intent of making great Italian cheese. "When we came here, it was kind of a new thing," Errico says. "They were mostly making cheddar here, and the first factory I bought was a little cheddar factory."

The reason he chose Wisconsin was because of the milk. "To make a good cheese, you need to be close to the cows," Errico says. "If I was in New York, I'd be close to the markets, but I'd rather be close to the cows, close to the source, close to the freshness. Everything comes together in the milk of Wisconsin."

When he first started making provolone, Parmesan, and other Italian specialty cheeses, most of his cheeses were exported out of the state, and most of them ended up on the East Coast. But over the last 20 years the tastes of the state and the nation have shifted, dramatically, and Wisconsin is now a great consumer of his cheeses. "There's been a tremendous change. Things have really changed so much that you don't even realize it," Errico says. "When I first moved here to the Green Bay area, I couldn't buy olive oil at the supermarket."

Today, Errico makes more than 20 different Italian specialties, from fresh mozzarella to

American Grana, an 18-month aged Parmesan. All of the cheeses are made from rBGH-free milk, and the cheeses are made by Errico and 20 different cheesemakers in five different plants in the Denmark and Pulaski area of Wisconsin. His company, though quite a bit larger than when he first started, remains committed to the same principles of excellence.

"You can't cut corners if you want to make a great cheese," Errico says. "If a cheese-maker is cutting corners, it can be anything from the aging temperature being a little off to using a cheaper enzyme. The cheese can be almost the same, but it's never quite as good. You have to really watch things carefully. Cheesemaking is affected by a thousand different variables, and if you're trying to make a perfect cheese, you have to keep an eye on it."

Errico loves cheese, and though he can wax poetic about the different and delicious cheeses he makes, he believes in the old-fashioned way of marketing. "The only way to describe cheese is to taste it," Errico says. "The name of a cheese doesn't tell the whole story, and to be fair to any specialty cheese, you have to taste them. If you believe in your product, just let people taste it."

Blaser's USA Inc.

1858 Highway 63

Comstock, WI 54826

715-822-2437

www.blasersusa.com

Italian Formaggio, Flavored Cheeses

The flowerpot is one of the original copper vats that were used to make cheese nearly a century ago..

While the original building of Blaser's USA hearkens back to the late 1800s, this little creamery sports a decidedly modern feel. At the same time, however, it maintains its depth of history.

A sunny little picnic area welcomes visitors, and in front of the creamery's offices, which originally were the cheesemaker's living quarters, a stunning copper pot is filled with flowers. That pot is actually one of the creamery's original copper vats, and it was used to make Swiss cheese. Stepping into the store, though, is like stepping into a roadside Tuscan deli. The side wall is lined with bottles of Italian wines, varieties that aren't imported anywhere else in the state, and the deli case is filled with imported hams and panini sandwiches and salads. There's even gelato and homemade fudge.

The creamery's first cheeses may have been Swiss, but it also has Italian roots. And it didn't start out as a cheese factory. When it began in 1901, it accepted home-separated cream from local farms, and then in 1907 the plant's owner sold it to a group of farmers who started the Comstock Cooperative Creamery. Comstock made butter and shipped it to Land O'Lakes Creamery in Minneapolis. The butter was trucked out of town on ice-packed railroad cars. In 1945, a Swiss-born cheesemaker named John Gurner purchased the business, and in 1948 his half-brother Herman Blaser, who came over from Switzerland, joined him. Herman Blaser was joined in his cheesemaking endeavor by another Herman, Herman Curella, the son of Italian immigrants. "Herman Blaser didn't speak a word of English when he came over," says Curella's son, Anthony, current owner of Blaser's. "When he first moved here, he lived at my father's farm."

Blaser bought the factory in 1959, and Anthony's father ran the plant. Anthony left northwest Wisconsin in 1963 to serve in the U.S. Air Force as a graphic illustrator. When he got out in 1972, he began working at a restaurant in Phoenix, and he helped grow the restaurant from a single location into a worldwide chain of 34 establishments. In 1991, Anthony returned to Comstock, Wisconsin, and he purchased the plant and began to grow it, just as he had helped the restaurant chain evolve.

"What started it all was the Blaser line, but at first, there really was no line," Anthony says. "I looked at our cheese, and I thought, 'Why can't we infuse flavors into them?' We were one of the first companies in the United States to do that, and some people thought we were nuts."

Their first flavor was a cranberry Muenster. That success led Anthony into creating additional lines of cheese, including the Antonella line of flavored semisoft cheeses. Inspired by the fine cheeses and flavors of Italy, they came up with a creamy formaggio base, which they then accented with ingredients such as capers and black peppercorns, garlic chive and spring dill, and scallions and crushed rosemary. The result is an attractive and delicious, yet approachable, line of cheeses that honors Anthony's family roots.

Their most recent addition to the fold is the Marcotte label, which features soft cheeses with a French, and exotic, twist, including flavors like pineapple ginger rolled in roasted coconut. Blaser also works with some even smaller cheese plants to help market their cheeses, including Castle Rock Organic Dairy and Holland's Family Farm. "They have to meet or exceed our standards," Anthony says. "You have to align yourself with quality."

CASTLE ROCK ORGANIC DAIRY

S13240 Young Road
Osseo, WI 54758
715 597-0085
www.castlerockfarms.net
CHEESE, MILK, ICE CREAM, BUTTER

Though Castle Rock Organic Dairy doesn't bill itself as a family operation, that's exactly what this small, northwestern Wisconsin creamery is. It all started when Wayne Kostka asked his friend Larry Julson to go for a ride to look at some dairy plants in Minnesota, because he was looking into developing one for his farm. "While we were at a dairy, we asked them, 'Do you know where we could purchase any of this equipment?' And they said, 'We know where there's a whole dairy,'" Larry recalls.

Wayne, Larry, and their whole families have gotten involved in the operations of the farm and the dairy. Wayne's wife, Carla, is the CEO; their son Barry and daughter-in-law Jeanne manage the farm and milking operations; and Larry's wife, Margaret, also is supportive. Indeed, photos of the Kostka's grandchildren and farm animals hang on the walls above the refrigerated case and the viewing windows of the creamery.

The organic farm was certified in 2000, the organic herd of cross-bred Holstein-Jersey cows was added in 2003, and the creamery went up in 2005. They first started with bottling milk and making ice cream, and then, in 2006, they began making cultured butter and cheese.

Though they've only been selling dairy products to customers for a couple years, this MOSA (Midwest Organic Services Association)-certified organic dairy has already developed quite a following, and with good reason. It has received 1150 points out of a possible 1200 points from the Cornucopia Institute, and their latest product, a signature blue cheese, is garnering rave reviews. "I'd put their blue up against any of them—it tastes better than Maytag blue," says Anthony Curella, who distributes the blue cheese.

COURTESY OF CASTLE ROCK ORGANIC DAIRY

At Castle Rock, the whole family gets involved in organic farming.

Larry, who is the cheesemaker and general plant manager, says they are pretty proud of that comparison. "Our blue cheese is one of a kind, and when we started this process, our main goal was to produce a wholesome product for consumers," Larry says.

The cows are all pasture grazed, and during the winter months when it is too cold to graze outside, they are fed with organic crops the owners grow themselves. After they made the decision to go completely organic, they started noticing some startling changes to the land and surrounding environment. "We started seeing songbirds in the old fence ways that had never been seen before," Barry says.

"We see species on our land that we don't see on our neighbors' property," Larry adds.

Barry, Larry, and the rest of the crew remain concerned about the watering down of organic farming. "It used to be that for a cow to be considered organic, it had to be raised from an organic cow and fed only organic feed," Larry says. "Now, you only have to feed cows organically for a year before you can call them organic. Now, what about the toxins that those cows might still have in their bodies before you switched the feed?"

At Castle Rock, everything is truly organic, and organic to the utmost degree. They don't, for example, use calcium chloride or other chemicals to help in the cheesemaking process. They don't need them—their milk is that good.

The milk is sold in glass bottles, but it also goes into their blue cheese, cheese curds, and their cheddarlike original, Harvest Moon cheese. It also goes into their ice cream, and they make 15 different flavors, including molasses chocolate chip, mint chocolate chip, cookies 'n cream, as well as several fruit varieties like strawberry, blueberry, and pumpkin spice. All of the ingredients for the ice cream are organic, and sometimes, they can be hard to find. "We needed two different cocoas for both the ice cream and the milk because some cocoas react differently when they are cold or hot," Larry says. "They're all fun to develop."

Besides dairy products, they also sell organic eggs, beef, and pork. Customers come to their farmstead store, but some receive delivery; their products are also sold at farmer's markets. Every year they host a customer appreciation day, and they give tours of their cheesemaking and milk bottling operations.

Because they are such a small operation, they've had to be self-sufficient, and Larry's electrical and engineering background (besides cheesemaking, he used to own a refrigeration repair business, an electrical business, and a machine shop) has come in handy. "Some days, you make the cheese, bottle the milk, fix the boiler, repair the bottle washer," Larry says. "When something breaks down, you could call someone, but by the time they come in, you've lost a day of production. All of the other businesses I had, they were easy compared to this."

HENNING'S CHEESE

20201 Ucker Point Creek Road
Kiel, WI 53042
920-894-3032
www.henningscheese.com
MAMMOTH CHEDDARS

*H*enning's Cheese is a small cheese company in Kiel that makes big cheeses. Big as in gigantic, not commodity. Cheese wheels that are 7 feet long and more than 6 feet wide; cheeses that start at 75 pounds, and have grown to sometimes as big as 54,000 pounds.

Mammoth cheddars they're called, and the head of this big cheese operation is Kerry Henning, a third generation master cheesemaker who, with his sister Kay Schmitz, runs the family cheese factory. Their grandfather, Otto Henning, started the company in 1914. "He made cheese for 49 years. Then my dad took over, and he's been making cheese for a mere 44 years," Kerry says, with an easy smile. "He still has a ways to go."

Kerry himself has only been making cheese for 25 years. The Hennings began making their trademark big cheese about 30 years ago after a client inquired about getting one. Word of their fine craftsmanship spread, and today they make big cheeses for stores around the country. The state of Texas, for example, has had quite an appetite for Kerry's big wheels.

Usually these giant cheeses are ordered to commemorate anniversaries, celebrate openings, or fete some other gala event. Sometimes they're even carved by a professional cheese sculptor. But they're show-stopping enough without any adornment. Often when they arrive at a store, there's a local television crew in tow, and sometimes the local television affiliates near Kiel show footage. "Then we'll get customers who call us to tell us, 'Your cheese was on TV,'" Kerry says with a laugh. "These cheeses really have that wow factor."

Sometimes Kerry will age these large cheeses for a year or longer. Sometimes the store managers will travel to Wisconsin to help make their cheese. If they're making an exceptionally large cheese, then they don't make their regular cheddars or Colbys. Instead, all of their rBGH-free milk, which comes from local farmers, goes toward the big cheese.

When Kerry's not making giant wheels, he's liable to be experimenting with different flavors and methods. His most recent achievement was to figure out the right technique in which to make crushed-peppercorn cheddar. For several years he tried making the cheese, but the cheese would crack. A trip to Italy—and a visit to some Pecorino, Romano, and other cheese factories—gave Kerry the inspiration he needed to solve the problem. "Now, I'm experimenting with shelf curing, and I'm trying out some different cultures," Kerry says. "You always keep on improving your art."

HOLLAND'S FAMILY CHEESE

N13851 Gorman Avenue

Thorp, WI 54771

715-669-5230

www.hollandsfamilycheese.com

RAW AND PASTEURIZED GOUDA, FLAVORED GOUDAS

*M*arieke Penterman and her husband, Rolf, first moved to Wisconsin so they could have a dairy farm of their own. Both had grown up on dairy farms in the Netherlands, but Rolf's father's little herd of 60 cows couldn't support his parents, his wife, and his brother Sander.

Farmland scarcity and government restrictions on how much they could grow their agricultural business in Holland led Rolf and Marieke to start scouring the globe for a good place to set up their own dairy farm. They looked elsewhere in Europe and Canada, but they chose Wisconsin after Sander had begun working at a farm in Baldwin, Wisconsin. Rolf, Marieke, and Sander purchased their Thorp farm in 2002. "We like Wisconsin," Rolf says. "The landscape is not too flat, and it's really a farm-friendly state. People really appreciate farmers here."

Although they liked Wisconsin and the dairy welcome they received, Marieke and Rolf really didn't like the cheese. Every time their family or friends came to visit them, they had them tuck a wheel or two of their beloved Dutch Gouda in their suitcases. That worked fine, until the airlines changed the weight regulations for suitcases, and their Dutch friends and family had to choose between packing clothes and packing cheese.

That got Marieke thinking. She already was looking into doing something on the farm that would allow her to work with her husband and care for their children (twins Joyce and Luna, their younger brother Dean, and another sibling currently on the way). The more she thought about it, the more she realized she could make authentic Gouda on their Wisconsin farm. She already knew she had the right quality of milk, and with some know-how and practice, she could do it. "We were addicted to the Netherlands' cheese," Marieke says. "We thought we could copy the recipe for real farmstead Gouda and make it here."

Marieke got her Wisconsin cheesemaker's license and also returned to Holland to work at a *boerenkaas,* or a Dutch farmstead cheese operation. She and Rolf imported all their cheesemaking equipment—the wooden shelves for aging the Gouda, the vats and brining tanks, along with all the cultures and spices.

After building the little creamery and store, Marieke finally began making cheese in November 2006. Less than six months after she first began making her Gouda, she won best of class for flavored semisoft cheese in the 2007 U.S. Cheese Championship for her foenugreek Gouda. Foenugreek is a sweet, almost maple syrup–like tasting seed, and it perfectly accents her sweet milk.

Marieke, along with the assistance of another cheesemaker, Dave Zakrzewicz, and two helpers, makes 13 different flavors of Gouda, as well as pasteurized and raw milk versions of her cheeses. She also ages her Goudas. Most Goudas made in the United States or imported from Holland are not aged Goudas. The majority of her Goudas are made from pasteurized milk because that's what her customers prefer, but Marieke personally favors the raw milk versions of her cheeses.

She makes about 300 pounds of cheese at a time, and she's still trying to discern for which flavors her customers have a preference. Marieke sells the cheese, along with Dutch and other European imports, including wooden shoes, from her farm store. By appointment, customers can also tour the farm from late spring until early fall. Viewing windows allow customers to see the cheeses being made, and allow them to peek in and watch the Goudas age.

Rolf and Sander tend to their herd of 630 Holsteins, who are not given chemicals or rBGH. The cows are housed in free-stall barns. About 10 to 20 percent of their milk goes into cheese production, and they sell the rest. If there's more demand for their cheeses, they might make more cheese. "You never know what the future holds," Marieke says. "It's unpredictable."

LoveTree Farmstead Cheese

12413 County Road Z

Grantsburg, WI 54840

715-488-2966

www.lovetreefarmstead.com

AMERICAN ORIGINAL CAVE-AGED SHEEP'S MILK CHEESES

(TRADE LAKE CEDAR, HOLMES SERIES, FISH BAIT)

Cheesemaker Mary Falk and her husband, David, are part mavericks and part trail-blazers, but they are 100 percent innovators. In fact, Mary is considered to be one of the most inventive and talented cheesemakers in the country, if not the world.

While Mary spent part of her childhood in Wisconsin, Mary's journey to become a Wisconsin cheesemaker started out in that western dairy state, California. Mary and her son Mitchell had come out to visit her parents at Christmas time. "I was just shocked at how gorgeous it was," Mary says. "On a lark, I went to a real estate company and started flipping through a book of available farmland. I found this place 10 miles north of my parents, and like a fool, I put an offer on it, with the contingency that I sell my cottage in Santa Cruz." Mary went back home, placed a FOR SALE sign on her lawn, and sold her little house in just one day. That was in 1986. A year later, after she had already begun transforming her land into an organic property, her neighbors coaxed her into meeting a friend, and that friend was David, whom she ended up marrying. They later had two additional sons, Charlie and Andy.

The family first started tending an organic flock of sheep in 1989, but it wasn't until 1993 that they got into the dairy industry. "Dave was building silos for grain storage, but that kept him off the farm five days a week. In order to preserve his sanity, he had to shut the company down," Mary says. "During this time, I had been in radio broadcasting, but I couldn't work anymore because of my asthma."

Mary and Dave went to visit a friend who lived 45 minutes south of them. This friend happened to be a sheep farmer, so he suggested that they milk their sheep. On their drive home, they wrote their business plan. "We decided that we couldn't be put in the position of other people paying us and telling us what our milk was worth, so we decided we would have to make our own cheese," Mary says. "There's no way that we could compete with the big boys, so we had to make something they couldn't—something like cave-aged, artisanal cheeses."

Mary had been making cheese as a hobby for 25 years, so she wasn't completely a novice when it came to aging dairy products, and she was particularly well versed in aging goat's milk cheeses. When Mary received her license, the original plan was to sell their milk until she had the right flavor profile she was seeking in her cheeses, and Dave had finished constructing their cave. That plan was abandoned after Dave became frustrated with the process of selling milk to others. "Dave came home from a meeting and pointed to my wicker basket of goat's milk cheeses, aging in the kitchen fireplace, and he said, 'Can you make that out of sheep's milk? You have two months, and by then I'll have the cave done,'" Mary says. "We had no one to ship our milk to, so it was sink or swim."

Fortunately for cheese lovers everywhere, Mary and Dave turned out to be excellent swimmers. Her first cheese, Trade Lake Cedar, an organic, raw sheep's milk cheese that's aged in caves on cedar bows, stunned cheese circles, winning several awards, including Best of Show at the American Cheese Society. Both Mary and Dave were named Food Artisans of the Year by *Bon Appetit*/Food Network.

Trade Lake Cedar led to several other cheeses, and all the cheeses get their distinct flavor from the milk of her Trade Lake sheep. These sheep, which have been bred for almost 20 years, hail from the stock of Clun Forest, Romney Marsh, and Dorset Horn sheep. The sheep, who only graze on grass, are hardy enough to survive winters in the North Woods. They are guarded by sheep dogs, who are also a carefully bred cross between Maremma and Spanish ranch mastiffs. These dogs' ancestors have guarded sheep in the rugged terrain of Spain for centuries, and Mary purchased them from Spanish shepherds. The dogs protect the sheep—

and also the chickens and other farm animals—from coyotes, wolves, bears, and other predators. "The dogs allow the wildlife to coexist with us," Mary says. "These dogs are amazing, and
they are guardians, not attack dogs. They will retreat to the flock, and they will only fight if
pushed."

Mary has sold some of her pups to ranchers and farmers throughout the country who
need to have their livestock protected. One rancher in Nevada, who previously shot 75 coyotes, has not had to kill a single predator in the year since his two dogs arrived. "The dogs
speak the wolves' language and the coyotes' language, and no predator likes to get caught
while sneaking up on a flock," Mary says. "The dogs really allow the wolves and the coyotes to
coexist with us because their packs avoid our animals."

Besides using cutting-edge conservation techniques to protect her flocks and the
wildlife, Mary continues to develop new cheeses. One of her most sought-after lines is
called Fish Bait. Because raw milk cheese is supposed to be aged for 60 or more days, this
cheese is legally sold as fish bait. "Our farmstead milk is four times cleaner than pasteurized
milk," Mary says. "I pull a sample for every batch of cheese to make sure it is safe."

With Fish Bait and her other cheeses, Mary attempts to capture the flavor of the woods
in northwestern Wisconsin. "When I walk through the woods up here, I don't feel sweet,"
Mary says. "Maybe for a short moment of spring with a flash of violets, but I see the spiciness,
the earthy smell of the woods, that pine and sumac spiciness and the floral that comes up in
gentle tones. That's what I try to play off of in my cheese."

SARTORI FOODS

107 Pleasant View Road

Plymouth, WI 53073

920-893-6061

www.sartorifoods.com

BELLAVITANO, ASIAGO, SARVECCHIO ASIAGO, SARVECCHIO PARMESAN, DOLCINA GORGONZOLA

In the little Italian town of Valdastico, just a few miles away from Asiago, Paul Sartori grew up feasting on fine Italian cheeses. So it's no surprise that when Paul and his family emigrated to the United States, he not only wanted to take those delicacies with him, but he also desired to bring his heritage of cheesemaking along, too. In 1939, just a few years after moving to Wisconsin, Paul founded S&R Cheese, now Sartori Foods, in Plymouth, a small village not unlike his hometown.

Nestled against the Kettle Moraine Forest, Plymouth proved to offer a similar climate and rural environs to his beloved northern Italy. Almost immediately after opening up shop, Paul started making Asiago; he also made Parmesan and other Italian varieties of cheese. In the late 1990s, his son Jim took over Sartori Foods.

Under Jim's guidance Sartori has kept up the standards Paul set, but he has also expanded the company. He's purchased other artisanal cheesemaking plants, including Antigo Cheese Company, and most recently the Glacier Point Artisan Cheese Company—both of which only employ handcrafted cheesemaking techniques. Antigo was known for its aged Parmesan, a Parmesan that *Bon Appetit* magazine considered to be the best domestic Parmesan. Glacier Point was known for its blue cheeses, including its newest, the particularly delectable Dolcina Gorgonzola.

Despite the expansions, the company remains family owned, and its team of master cheesemakers remains true to Paul's original goal of bringing fine Italian cheeses to the

American table. In fact, they still use many of the same recipes Paul created, but the cheese-makers have also worked to develop new and interesting cheeses, including the stunning Bellavitano.

"We're known for labor-intensive, handcrafted cheeses," says Liz Bowes, marketing manager. "We call Bellavitano 'the indescribable cheese' because of its addictive craveablity. We actually have people hunt us down after tasting it, and then they buy it by the case if they can't find it in their local grocery stores."

SAXON CREAMERY

855 Hickory Street
Cleveland, WI 53015
920-693-8500
www.saxoncreamery.com

TRAPPIST/WASHED RIND CHEESES

The Saxon Creamery is one of Wisconsin's newest farmstead artisans, and the creamery was more than a decade in the making on this more than century-old farm in Manitowoc County.

The genesis started back in 1991 when the Klessig family began their journey from conventional dairy farming into rotational grazing. The family—Robert and Kathleen Klessig, Karl and Liz Klessig, and Jerry Heimerl and Lisse Klessig Heimerl, all the fifth generation of Klessigs to run the dairy farm—had just heard about rotational grazing. They didn't know anyone in the Midwest who was doing it, so they sent Robert out to New Zealand to see what it was all about. Robert came back on fire for the idea, so the first step was to see if their cows actually wanted to go outside.

After being coaxed out into the field, the cows had this look of natural joy on their faces, and the Klessigs were sold. "A crippled cow who had trouble walking in the barn was running in the fields within a couple of weeks," says Dan Strongin, one of the consultants the Klessigs hired to help open their creamery. "That was their epiphany, that was the moment that started it."

That was the first step, and the latest step was taken in 2007 when they finally opened their environmentally friendly, virtually organic creamery. Today, the cows are found in the pasture except on the very coldest and snowiest days of the year (they hate to be in their barns), and they're grass fed for as long as they can forage for grass.

The whole creamery is set up around environmentally friendly practices, and they try to recycle whenever possible. In fact, they don't package their cheeses in plastic like most cheesemakers. They use breathable, resealable packaging. They also have applied to be the first creamery to be certified Green Tier, a special environmental certification in the state.

"What they are showing is that well-run family farms are the best environmental defense," Strongin says. "This is why I got involved to help them."

WIDMER CHEESE CELLARS

214 Henni Street

Theresa, WI 53091

888-878-1107

www.widmerscheese.com

BRICK, AGED CHEDDAR, AND COLBY

Joe Widmer makes cheese just the way his father and his grandfather did.

Cream city bricks are stacked in a line against the back wall of Widmer Cheese Cellars. Joe Widmer carefully removes a brick from the shelf and tilts it onto its side to reveal a faded imprint of a stamp, showing that it was made nearly a century ago. "My grandfather used these," Joe says, placing the brick back on the white shelf.

Joe still uses those same bricks—the bricks that both his grandfather John O. Widmer and his father, John J. Widmer, used. Those bricks press the curds into cheese forms, and they're flipped three times the first day that they are made. Though Joe has added such modern accoutrements as computers and air-conditioning to his small plant in Theresa, Wisconsin, he uses the same recipes and most of the same equipment that his grandfather used. A stickler for tradition, he remains the only cheesemaker in America to make brick cheese the old-fashioned way.

"Brick is actually an American original cheese," Joe says. "It was actually created by a Swiss cheesemaker in the 1870s, not more than 20 minutes up the road from us."

Joe's grandfather was also a Swiss immigrant, who came to Wisconsin to apprentice to cheesemakers in 1905. He started his own cheesemaking operation in 1918, moving it to

Theresa in 1922. His grandfather lived upstairs from the plant. Joe grew up in those same quarters, and until 1998, he and his family lived there, too. "Though my grandfather was Swiss, he made a German-style cheese because that's what the market wanted," Joe says.

Back then, when his grandfather started making cheese, there were 140 cheesemakers in Dodge County alone. Now, there are only a handful of cheese factories in Dodge County, and of those, Joe's is the only one whose cheese is crafted by hand.

It's no wonder then, that Joe's cheeses, his brick, his aged cheddars, and his Colby, have won numerous national and international awards. His award-winning brick is mixed into a savory brick cheese spread, too. The awards are displayed on the wall in his tiny office. It is here that Joe also receives the e-mails and letters from fans. "Your brick cheese is the best I've ever tasted," reads one e-mail from a fan in California.

The letters and the visitors come from all over the country, and occasionally, the world. When visitors tour the plant, they not only can enjoy the aged cheeses Joe is known for, but they can also taste warm, just made cheddar curds—the kind that squeak against your teeth as you chew them. "You can look back at the end of the day and see that you've accomplished something," Joe says.

Wisconsin cheeses come in a rainbow of delicious hues. CLOCKWISE FROM CENTER: *Chalet Cheese Cooperative's Baby Swiss, on top of Roth Käse aged Gouda, on top of Sartori Foods' aged Parmesan; Roth Käse aged Gouda, Chalet Cheese Cooperative's Limburger on top of Uplands Cheese Company's Pleasant Ridge Reserve; Montforte Gorgonzola, Widmer's aged Brick, Crave Brothers' Les Frères Homestead, Roth Käse Gran Queso, Roth Käse Gruyère, Roth Käse Knight's Vail, and Roth Käse Cave-Aged Cheddar.*

LEFT: *Crave Brothers' fresh mozzarella makes a perfect Caprese salad—just mozzarella, tomatoes, and basil, drizzled with a little virgin olive oil and perhaps an olive or two for garnish.* ABOVE: *Wisconsin offers a wide variety of blues including BelGioioso Creamy Gorgonzola, Roth Käse Buttermilk Blue, Seymour Dairy AderKase, Montforte Gorgonzola, and Maple Leaf True Blue Cheddar.*

ABOVE: *Les Frères is the signature cheese of Crave Brothers.* TOP RIGHT: *Sid Cook at Carr Valley Cheese creates wide selection of mixed milk cheeses including Menage, Shepherd's Blend, Gran Canaria, Benedictine, and Mellage.* BOTTOM RIGHT: *Carr Valley's Monastery, Cocoa Cardona, Cave-Aged Cheddar, and Creama Kasa.* PHOTOS © 2007 WISCONSIN MILK MARKETING BOARD, INC.

CLOCKWISE FROM CENTER: *Roth Käse Cave-Aged Cheddar, Carr Valley Applewood Smoked Cheddar, Roth Käse Gruyère, Upland's Cheese Company's Pleasant Ridge Reserve, Roth Käse Aged Gouda, Bel-Gioioso's Manteche (mild provolone), BelGioioso Pepato, BelGioioso Creamy Gorgonzola, and Roth Käse Buttermilk Blue.* PHOTO © 2007 WISCONSIN MILK MARKETING BOARD, INC.

Many children in Wisconsin grow up on string cheese. Crave Brothers' string cheese and rope cheese are among the best. PHOTO © 2007 WISCONSIN MILK MARKETING BOARD, INC.

The milk for Crave Brothers' fresh mozzarella, mascarpone, and rope cheeses come directly from the brothers' farm across the street from the factory. PHOTO © 2007 WISCONSIN MILK MARKETING BOARD, INC.

CHAPTER 6

Other Dairy Masters of
WISCONSIN
(Including Yogurt, Ice Cream, Butter, and Milk)

BLUE MARBLE DAIRY

7571 Kirch Road
Barneveld, WI 53507
608-924-2721
www.bluemarblefamilyfarm.com
MILK, CREAM, CHOCOLATE MILK, AND SMOOTHIES

*N*ick Kirch grew up in a dairy farming family, and when he first took over the family farm from his father, he continued to sell his milk to others who would bottle it or use it for cheese. But after the FDA approved the use of synthetic bovine growth hormone, or rBGH, in 1992, Nick started thinking that he didn't want to be on that road, and he began to look at alternatives, including setting up his own farmstead bottling operation. "It just didn't seem to be a good thing," Nick says. "The reason I came up with the idea of what I'm doing is I'm against 'get bigger at any cost,' and that's the direction farming was headed."

For the next decade, Nick really didn't do much more than mull the idea over. Then, in 2003, against the advice of other farmers and bigger milk companies, he started putting his plans together. It took three more years to come up with the building, financing, and marketing plans, not to mention just getting his paperwork in order. Since milk is a Grade A product, Nick needed to purchase all Grade A–certified equipment, and most of the modern bottling equipment is only made for larger milking operations. That added to the difficulty. Nick, for example, thought that a commercial dishwasher would be perfect to sanitize his glass bottles, but federal regulations forbid the use of a cleaning machine that wasn't specifically created for milk bottles. "They don't make them anymore," Nick says, pointing toward his antique bottle washer, which was built in the 1950s. "I tracked that down in Utah and had it refurbished."

Nick began his bottling operations in May 2006, milking his herd of 80 cows and bottling about 400 quarts the first month. A year later, he was bottling 10,000 quarts and still growing. Nick started working with local stores and the West Side Farmer's Market in Madison. Then, he teamed up with Sugar River Yogurt and other organic producers to deliver milk, yogurt, cheese, and produce directly to consumers in the region.

Today he sells whole milk, skim milk, chocolate milk, and cream, and he also sells smoothies. Nick has plans to develop some coffee drinks, and he would also like to set up a small petting zoo and retail shop at his farm, but those plans are a year or two away from being actualized.

Since Nick's milk is not homogenized, he's had to educate his customers about how to shake the bottles to reconstitute the cream into the milk. "When they homogenize milk, they put it under 4,000 pounds of pressure to break down the butterfat," Nick says. "That changes the enzymes and the composition of the milk. What I've discovered is that some of my customers thought they were lactose intolerant, but they can drink my milk without any problems. It turns out they only had digestive problems with homogenized milk."

Nick is still working on expanding his customer base, and he would like to distribute his dairy products to more stores. As a single father, he wants to make sure that his farm is sustainable, and that he could pass it on to his two sons, Johann and Keller.

CAPRINE SUPREME

W5646 Highway 54

Black Creek, WI 54106

920-984-3388

GOAT'S MILK YOGURT AND CHEESE

A chance encounter at the Outagamie County Fair led Todd and Sheryl Jaskolski into the realm of goat's milk yogurt. "We were showing our goats, and an older lady came up to me and said, 'How come there isn't anybody making goat's milk yogurt?'" Todd recalls. "I thought, 'There's an idea.'"

That was an idea that didn't let go of Todd, so he and Sheryl investigated it further, discovering that just one company on the West Coast was making goat's milk yogurt. "I tasted it, and I thought, 'We can do better than this,'" Todd says.

So they set about experimenting and working with CC's Jersey Crème, and they developed a formula for goat's milk yogurt, coming up with a good blended recipe. Along the way, Todd also received his cheesemaker's license, and in 2007 they completed construction of their farmstead creamery in an old garage that was remodeled to suit their needs.

Their yogurt offers a natural sweetness that comes from the quality of goat's milk, a quality that even some state inspectors have marveled at. Sheryl is in charge of the goats, and she babies her herd. "It's really Sheryl," Todd says. "She has a way with goats. I would put our goats up against any other goats in the state."

Sheryl's goats—a mix of Saanen, Alpine, and Nubian—are allowed to freely wander inside and outside of their barns. They're even given outside access during the winter, which, believe it or not, they enjoy. They also are allowed to "mow" the pastures, but although they do a good job of trimming the grass down, they don't always want to return to their regular roaming area.

Right now, Todd is working to develop a line of fresh chèvres and has plans to work on some aged cheeses. He also would like to bottle the goat's milk right there on the farm. "I like to cook, and it's a lot like cooking," Todd says. "We just try to offer the freshest, highest quality of milk there is."

CRYSTAL BALL ORGANIC FARMS

At Crystal Ball, milk is bottled right on the farm.

CRYSTAL BALL ORGANIC FARMS

527 State Road 35
Osceola, WI 54020
715-294-4090

MILK, CREAM, ICE CREAM, BUTTER, CHEESE CURDS

Troy and Barb DeRosier had not planned on starting their own farmstead milk bottling and ice cream plant. But when their oldest son, Jared, was born in 1998, he had quite severe physical and mental challenges. "We realized that we are going to need to provide for him for the rest of his life," Troy says. "We needed a more solid source of income."

They had already been organically farming with their small herd of 100 cows, so they began the process of setting up an organic milk plant. By bottling their own milk, they would be able to better support their son. They decided to go with glass bottles, selling non-homogenized, cream line milk because of the health benefits, and their first line of products included skim, 2 percent, and whole milk, as well as cream and half-and-half. The milk is gently pasteurized and bottled, going from the cow to the customers within 48 hours. "Our milk has a sweet taste, and our milk arrives at our customers fresher," Troy says. "With more conventionally processed milk, milk arrives at customers several days after the cows initially are milked."

Troy has a small staff who helps him with the operations of the creamery and the farm, but his most eager helper is his four-year-old son Jordan. "He's my shadow," Troy says.

After Crystal Ball's milk began developing a following throughout Wisconsin, Troy added butter and cheese curds to the mix, and then, in the summer of 2006, he began making ice cream and yogurt smoothies. His ice cream flavors include chocolate–peanut butter, buttermilk blueberry, banana, cookies 'n cream, coffee, strawberry, and mint chip. He's also been working with the University of Wisconsin–River Falls to develop other flavors, and he'd eventually like to make some aged cheeses. "With cheese, it's quite an art," Troy says. "But cheese curds are more forgiving and not as fussy."

About a third of their customers receive their milk through a home delivery program, and Troy teams up with other local and organic producers of meat, honey, and produce to bring these staples right to customers' homes. Other customers pick up their milk and dairy products at their Osceola farm store, and some distributors take their milk throughout the state and also to Minnesota and Illinois.

Every year Troy and Barb host a free, special kids' day at their farm for children with special needs and their families. The first year about 200 people came, and the event now attracts a crowd of more than 600. Though Troy and Barb hosted the first event by themselves, local businesses and volunteers have gotten involved. The barns are opened, hay and pony rides are offered, and a pig roast is held. They also set up fun games for children, including a bouncing castle and a soy bean pit that they can jump in. "A lot of kids love that," Troy says. "Soy beans have a different feel to them, and disabled kids really like that."

Parents also really appreciate the farm day because it's something they can enjoy with both their disabled children and the rest of the family. "We know how hard it is for these families to find events to do for the whole family, not just their disabled children," Troy says. "This is really for the whole family."

DAVIS FARM

North 5026 County J
Kennan, WI 54537
715-474-3454
MILK, CREAM

A good deal on farmland led John and Judy Davis to move across country, from Washington state to Kennan, Wisconsin, and a bad break on milk prices led them to start their own bottling operation.

Their Wisconsin journey starts, however, in 1991, when they first moved to the farm, learning upon their arrival why the cost had been so reasonable. The farm's house and out-buildings were a little bit run-down, to say the least. "The house wasn't fit to house hound dogs," John says. "When we first moved here, my wife cried for three days. She was sobbing, bawling, and then she took our pickup truck and went to the village. She came back with cleaning supplies and went to work. Look at what she's done."

"The first check I wrote was for $15, and it was for cleaning supplies," says Judy, show-ing the line in her old check registry, where she wrote "cleaning supplies" in the ledger.

Judy and John set to work fixing up the property, and with more than a little determina-tion, they transformed the land and buildings into a pastoral farmstead. Besides the draft horses they brought with them to plow the land, they added cows and chickens, and when their triplets—Joey, Justin, and Jacob—were born, a neighbor gave them three bunnies and three goslings. John built a special hutch for the bunnies, but the bunnies dug holes so they could come and go as they pleased. One original bunny still is alive, and he hangs out in the hutch, but visitors can occasionally glimpse his offspring of dark colored, little rabbits. "They're fast, but the boys can catch them," Judy says.

Milk pricing in 2000 led them into their next venture. That's when milk prices dropped, and John decided that instead of getting 60 cents for every dollar of milk from government subsidies, he would start a bottling plant. "I realized that I was addicted to farming, and there's no 12-step program for that," John says.

So John and Judy began their journey into milk bottling. John found a company in Canada that still made bottles, and he requested a sample of different bottle caps. He used the caps to track down defunct farmstead bottling operations to get both advice and old equipment. "I found people who know how to do this, and their advice to us was always not to do this," John says.

Bits and pieces of equipment started trickling in, from Pennsylvania, Ohio, and New York, among other places. Unfortunately, a lot of the equipment was as defunct as the old bottling plants that it came from—rusted and broken. "It was junk," John says. The first government inspectors who came out to their farm just scratched their heads, not believing that John or Judy would make it.

But John was able to transform that "junk" into a beautiful little creamery. Today they sell milk, cream, eggs, meat, and vegetables from their little farmstead store. They're not certified organic because they don't want to have to pass that cost of being certified on to their customers, but they don't use any chemicals, additives, or hormones—they don't even use tractors—and their small herd of about a dozen cows grazes naturally. Because their milk is of such a high quality, every few months a rabbi comes out to kosher certify the milk, and he takes some back with him to Minnesota.

Most of their customers come to their small farmstead store, but a local man has started a delivery service, and he's taking their milk and cream to customers. "It's growing, and I'm happy with that," John says.

Their experience has benefited other small artisanal creameries, including Castle Rock Organic Dairy. "He really gave us some good advice," says Larry Julson, cheesemaker and plant manager. "John told us how it really was."

SIBBY'S ORGANIC ICE CREAM

Viroqua Public Market/Sibby's Organic Zone Ice Cream Parlor

215 South Main Street

Viroqua, WI 54665

608-637-1912

www.sibbysicecream.com

ICE CREAM

*S*ue "Sibby" Huber grew up on a dairy farm, but she never dreamed of making her living from dairy, much less making ice cream. In fact, for almost two decades, she drove a United Parcel Service (UPS) truck.

Her journey back to her dairy roots started in 1990 when she purchased her family's original homestead farm, which at the time had been pretty neglected. "I always thought I wanted to share that kind of life with my children," Sibby says.

That kind of life included a vision of turning the broken down farmstead into an organic pasture. She set to work immediately, rebuilding the old Norwegian barn and the silos. When she left UPS in 1998, she was able to put more attention to restoration, especially since she was living in a trailer on the property. It took her, a single mother, one and a half years to construct a new home, using recycled and green materials. Around the same time she ran into one of her trucker buddies, and she asked how the Veroqua Dairy was doing, since the dairy had been on one of her delivery routes. "He told me things were slow," Sibby says. "So I told him to tell Tim, the manager, that he should make some organic ice cream."

Tim didn't end up making organic ice cream himself, but he did teach Sibby the basics of ice cream making, and Sibby started thinking that maybe her future was in dairy after all. Sibby began taking some entrepreneurial classes and working with consultants to come up with her own recipes for organic vanilla and organic chocolate ice cream. "Those classes were good for me," she says. "When you start thinking of such things as packaging and UPC codes, to finding ingredients and keeping your books straight, it's almost impossible, and I don't know how I did it."

Finally, in June 2003, she made her first 4,000 pounds of ice cream, and after she packed up 200 pints in a little freezer hooked up to a generator in the back of her truck, Sibby drove down to Madison to begin selling her product. "I came home with 190 pints," Sibby says, with a laugh. "But then they called me, and slowly things grew. After the first pint went onto a shelf at a little food co-op, I took a look at it, and I said to myself, 'Okay, it's been done.' Well, that was just the beginning, sister."

Today, Sibby, with the help of just two part-time employees, a bookkeeper who works from home, and her teenage sons Ross and Joe, makes about 4,000 pounds of ice cream each month, all from scratch at her certified organic plant down at her farm. She also runs Sibby's Organic Zone Ice Cream Parlor in Viroqua with her partner, Dr. Tony Macaset. The parlor, which is the only organic ice cream parlor in the country, serves up her vanilla and chocolate ice creams, topped with organic fudge and cashew crunch candies made by some local Amish friends of hers.

Sibby loves her cows just as much as she loves her ice cream.

"It's really the American dream to create something and to get off that corporate merry-go-round," Sibby says. "I want people to be able to look at what I've done and say, 'If she can do it, I can do it, too.'"

SUGAR RIVER YOGURT

N7346 County Highway D
Albany, WI 53502
608-938-1218
YOGURT

Chris Paris credits her husband, Ron, with getting them into the yogurt-making business. Ron blames his brother Bert, whose pasture-grazed cows produce milk for Edelweiss Creamery's delectable cheeses.

"Back in November 1999, he took me to a conference about value-added dairy," Ron explains. "At that conference, I met a spokesperson for yogurt-making equipment from Israel. I thought, 'Here we are, the Dairy State, and no one's making yogurt.'"

That got Ron and Chris pondering the possibilities, and before long they decided to go for it. Though Ron had grown up on a farm, neither he nor Chris worked directly in the dairy business. So they did a lot of research, and they discovered that unlike cheese plants, which are Grade B dairy production facilities, yogurt requires a Grade A license. It took more than two years of hard work and negotiating sticky red tape to get their business up and running.

"We're so small, and nothing is geared for small," Chris says. "What we are doing is part of a newer movement, and there aren't many small artisans. When you are a small company that has to fit the larger corporate requirements, it's challenging. We had a lot of inspectors ask us, 'Are you sure you want to do this?' They almost wanted to talk us out of it because there are so many regulations."

The couple, who live near the scenic Sugar River, was finally able to negotiate all of the regulations. Their yogurt operation is now attached to their garage, where, in one small, white, and immaculately clean room, they make plain, vanilla, and fruit-on-the-bottom flavors including blueberry, peach, raspberry, and strawberry. Because there aren't any in-state fruit processors, all their fruit has to come from California. Right now, they're working on a

Chris and Ron Paris show off some freshly-made yogurt

grant to see if they can help some state fruit farmers grow and process local fruits, like elder-berries and perhaps seaberries. "We're experimenting to see how these fruits work with dairy products," Ron says.

Their milk comes from two local farmers who pasture-graze and do not give their cows any hormones. Because the milk arrives unhomogenized, the resulting yogurt has a velvety, custardlike texture and a creaminess that belies its low-fat nature. "We just want our yogurt to be the best it can be," Chris says.

Phillip Tetzner, his wife, and grandson stand outside their self-service store

TETZNER DAIRY

30455 Nevers Road
Washburn, WI 54891
715-373-2330
FARMSTEAD MILK, CREAM, ICE CREAM, ICE CREAM SANDWICHES

With a view of Lake Superior through the bluffs and trees, Tetzner Dairy offers perhaps the most scenic view of any milk bottling plant in the country. If not, it certainly is the most northern dairy in the state, since it is located in Washburn, near Bayfield, which is one of the most northern points in Wisconsin.

And calling Tetzner Dairy a milk bottling plant is a bit of a misnomer. Though milk is bottled and ice cream is made there, Tetzner Dairy is a family farmstead operation with a herd of just 100 Holsteins. This beautiful little country dairy was started by Phillip Tetzner, who's been in the dairy business his entire life. "My dad drove a milk route," Phillip explains. "My dad got sick, so when I was 12 years old, I got my license [to deliver milk], and my mother drove the truck."

When Phillip was 18 years old, his father died, so he took over the milk delivery business and the family farm, which at the time had five cows. He grew his herd, and he sold raw milk right from the farm. But in 1976 the state laws changed, so Phillip decided to set up a farmstead bottling operation. "If I had planned to sell all of our milk through the farm operation, it would have been a problem," Phillip says. "I just figured that we would make it if we sold 100 gallons a day."

Tetzner Dairy did just that—and then some—and in 1986, after Phillip decided to bottle skim milk, he needed to do something with his leftover cream, so he began to make ice cream on the farm, too. Today, he works with his son Greg and his two grandsons, Matt and Peter. Phillip is in charge of all the bookkeeping, and he still makes the ice cream, which they then make into ice cream sandwiches by hand, too.

His wife of 58 years, Beverly Jean, also helps. "This is Beverly Jean, the jelly bean," Phillip says, with a twinkle in his eye and a smile.

"I am not a jelly bean," Beverly Jean says, setting him straight with a hint of a smile.

Customers serve themselves at the farm store, which also sells cheese, soda, and a few other items. After purchasing their milk and ice cream, they can linger and visit with some of the farm animals, including the pet goats and dogs, who often greet visitors. "The milk is all fresh," Phillip says. "Bottling fresh milk is one of our secrets. Most of the milk in stores is at least a week old. Here, it's not, and our prices are competitive. And everybody likes ice cream."

The ice cream comes in several flavors, including cherry nut, peppermint, and chocolate mint, and every December they also make peppermint with chocolate chips. They make the sandwiches all by hand, molding the ice cream in Tupperware containers before cutting it to fit the chocolate wafers. "Those are really popular," Phillip says.

Phillip Tetzer's dairy operation is a lot smaller than this factory.

Joseph and Bernadine started the Weber Dairy on their family farm.

WEBER DAIRY

9706 County Road H
Marshfield, WI 54449
715-384-5639

FARMSTEAD MILK, CREAM, EGGNOG

Weber's Farm Store has stood on the corner of County Road H and Lincoln Avenue, on the outskirts of Marshfield, for more than a half century, and the store sits on a farm that dates back even further, to 1904.

For more than a century, the Weber family has farmed in northwest Wisconsin, and today the farm is run by Joellen Heiman and her husband, Ken, along with Ken's brothers Kelvin and Kim, who also run the Nasonville Dairy cheese factory. They took over the farm and dairy in 1995.

The farm was founded by Joellen's great-grandfather Peter Weber, and it then passed on to her grandfather John, and then on to her parents, Joseph and Bernadine. Her parents were the ones who started the store in 1955; prior to setting up the store, Joseph would deliver raw milk and cream door-to-door. Customers used to bring in their own containers to fill up with milk until the state law changed in 1959. That's when the Webers started to bottle milk, and then, in 1973, they switched to a plastic-bag system. Milk is bottled in plastic bags, which then are set into plastic pitchers.

What makes the Weber Farm Store unique, besides the fact that they produce their own rBGH-free milk and cream on-site, is that most customers don't walk into the little store; instead, they use the drive-through to pick up their fresh milk, along with locally grown meats, eggs, cheese, and ice cream. Joellen makes soft-serve ice cream sundaes and ice cream pies—customers adore her Moolicious ice cream pies, which are made with fudge, caramel, and toffee—and the farm bottles juice drinks, too. "A lot of people have never seen people drive up to get a gallon of milk, and they're just amazed," says Joellen. "It's a lot like McDonald's, but we don't have french fries and hamburgers. We have dairy products."

Joellen and Ken's sons, Josh and Ryan, help out on the farm. Josh is the main person in charge with the crops—they grow the food their small herd of 265 cows (130 are milking cows) eat—and Ryan helps with the crops, too. Their daughter Michelle is a teacher. "I think my parents are proud of us," Joellen says. "It's really unique, and my parents' dream was to establish a business that could carry on to the next generation."

Visitors can pick up their live bait for fishing at the drive-through window, but they can also stop and tour the calves' barn, where they can go right up to the little cows, which will lick their fingers if given a chance. In the summer, they might get to visit with the farm kittens, too. "People can walk right in to pet the calves or kittens, and our customers are just fascinated," Joellen says.

Weber's makes whole milk, 2 percent, 1 percent, no fat (skim), 2 percent chocolate, and heavy cream. Every winter, though, they also make a reduced-fat eggnog, which is quite popular with their customers.

But the busiest season for the store is the summer months, and on some days it's not uncommon to see lines of cars stretched out through the parking lot. Most of their customers are local, but they also receive a fair amount of tourists, along with people who have come to Marshfield to go for treatments at the Marshfield Clinic. Because their store isn't open on Sundays or holidays, they also sell their milk and cream to local stores throughout the area. "We're almost always busy," Joellen says.

CHAPTER 7

The Artisanal and Specialty
COW CHEESES

CRAVE BROTHERS FARMSTEAD CHEESE

LES FRÈRES

Robust, earthy, and bursting with flavor, this washed rind cheese is reminiscent of the famed French St. Nec-taire, but it is a cheese unique to Waterloo, Wisconsin. This American original washed rind cheese offers a slightly nutty tang with a sweet, almost creamy undertone, and it's no wonder that it has taken several national and international awards, including winning the silver medal in its category in the 2005 World Cheese Competition. Les Frères comes in big, 2-pound wheels or the more

Crave Brothers Farmstead Cheese, Les Frères

delicate, 8-ounce Petit Frère. Also delicious are the Crave Brothers' fresh mozzarella, fresh rope, and fresh mascarpone. The mascarpone is particularly sweet and incredibly delicious.

HENNING'S CHEESE

MAMMOTH CHEDDARS/FLAVORED CHEDDARS

Henning's mammoth cheddars are a bit harder for individuals to come by—unless you live near a store that happens to have a 1,000-pounder displayed. Their flavor is a bit more intense, and different from a typical cheddar. Although the big cheeses are hard to come by, Henning's flavored cheddars are easy for individuals to order. My favorite flavor is the crushed peppercorn. This mild, white cheddar boasts just the right amount of spice to make this an amazing cheese. Also quite good is the award-winning sun-dried tomato and basil cheddar. Both cheeses are great for snacking, but also perfect for grilled cheese sandwiches.

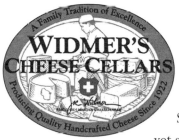

WIDMER'S CHEESE CELLARS

BRICK

Strong in flavor yet soft in texture, this is real brick cheese. Aged for three months in the cellar, its washed rind packs in a punch of flavor. Earthy yet slightly sweet, Joe Widmer's brick is something best savored alone or perhaps on a slice of pumpernickel bread. For those whose palates prefer milder flavors, he also makes a specialty brick that isn't quite as pungent. Joe also makes a divine aged brick cheese spread that is very flavorful.

AGED CHEDDAR

Joe Widmer also is a master at creating aged cheddars of up to nine years. His cheddar is the only American cheddar carried in stock at the Ideal Cheese Company in New York City, and it's easy to taste why. Strong, nicely textured, and full-bodied, Joe's cheddars are real cheddars, and there's nothing sissy about them.

COLBY

Joe Widmer also makes a great Colby—real Colby, mind you, not the light cheddars that masquerade as Colby on most grocery store shelves. Mild and sweet, this Colby comes plain or in a tangy vegetable flavor, too. It's easy on the palate and quite good.

UPLANDS CHEESE COMPANY

PLEASANT RIDGE RESERVE

The nutty and richly nuanced Pleasant Ridge Reserve reminds one of the Beaufort Alpine mountain cheese found in the southeastern region of France, but this cheese reigns in a world all its own. An American original, this aged, unpasteurized, and washed rind cheese is made entirely from the milk of pasture-grazing cows. Similar to a Gruyère, it offers

© 2007 WISCONSIN MILK MARKETING BOARD, INC.

Uplands Cheese Company Pleasant Ridge Reserve

layer upon layer of distinct flavor, and it's no wonder that it is one of the most decorated American cheeses. Most significantly, it took Best of Show championship honors from the American Cheese Society competition not once, but twice, in 2001 and 2005, making it only the second cheese in the country to accomplish that feat. The 6-month aged version is milder than its 17-month aged counterpart.

SARTORI FOODS

BELLAVITANO

No one else makes Bellavitano, and though it is considered an American original, it's patterned after northern Italian farmstead cheeses. Aged for several months, Bellavitano has the crystalline crunch of a fine Gruyère, but it tastes more like a crumbly Parmesan, except that it's creamier than Parmesan ever gets. Sweet, with just a hint of an edge to it, it goes down quite easily.

SARVECCHIO ASIAGO

This is an aged and brined cheese that you could easily confuse with an Italian import. Sweet, crumbly, and delicious, it goes great with pasta, bread, and all by itself. Also quite delectable is the SarVecchio Parmesan.

DOLCINA GORGONZOLA

This is a sweet, creamy blue with just the right amount of bite. It's great spread on a piece of bread, and it's also delicious served with port wine.

EDELWEISS TOWNHALL CREAMERY

EMMENTALER

Unless you travel to Switzerland, you can't find Swiss cheese that's this fresh. Made the traditional way, in 180-pound wheels, this Emmentaler cheese is created using raw milk and blending it in a traditional copper vat (which cheesemaker Bruce Workman purchased from a Switzerland cheesemaking school that was going out of business). It is,

in fact, the only Swiss cheese made in 180-pound wheels in the United States. The cheese itself is a serious cheese, packed full of flavor. It's wonderful sliced and served with apples or pears, but it also makes an amazing fondue.

GRASS-FED GOUDA

It's hard to get a Gouda that's sweeter than Bruce Workman's. Made entirely from the milk of rotationally grazed cows, this honey-gold colored beauty boasts a subtle nuttiness, and the lushness of the pasture comes through. Clean on the palate, it's an all-around great cheese for noshing, especially with apples. It also happens to be the favorite cheese of Edelweiss partner and farmer Bert Paris, whose cows provide the milk for the cheese.

Bruce Workman shows off two wheels of his Gouda

K & K CHEESE / NATURAL VALLEY CHEESE

KNAPP'S VALLEY

When I first tried this cheese, master cheesemaker Tom Torkelson didn't even have a name for it yet. It didn't need a name this cave-aged, semi soft, washed rind beauty was in a class all its own. Made with milk from Amish farms, this cheese is as natural as can be. Earthy, strong, and oh-so-good, Knapp's Valley isn't for cheese neophytes. But for those who like good cheese, this American original packs a punch of flavor, and it tastes great with a glass of Beaujolais.

K & K–NATURAL VALLEY CHEESE / BRUNKOW / CARR VALLEY / BASS LAKE

JUUSTOLEIPA

Traditionally, in Scandinavian countries, Juustoleipa is made with reindeer's milk. In each of these Wisconsin versions, Juusto is made from cow's milk. What makes this cheese unusual is not just its taste, but its texture. It's a caramelized cheese that looks like bread, and unlike other cheeses that get all gloppy and melty, it retains its basic, spongy structure even if you grill it, nuke it in the microwave, or cook it over an open flame. Each of these Wisconsin cheesemakers puts his own stamp on Juusto, and they're all quite decadent and delicious,

Tom Torkelson and Bentley Lein show off some of Tom's aged beauties.

especially dipped in jam, salsa, or ranch dressing.

HOOK'S CHEESE COMPANY

SWEET CONSTANTINE

Tony and Julie Hook like to experiment, and this is their homage to Italian cheeses. Similar to a Parmesan, but made with whole, not skim, milk, Sweet Constantine is a sharp, tangy delight. Salty and strong, this American original crumbles easily, making it a perfect pasta topper. It also tastes amazing with a little drizzle of aged balsamic vinegar.

COLBY

Most caseophiles consider Colby to be passé, but when it's done right, it's done right, and the Hooks do it right. In fact, Julie became the first woman ever to win the American Cheese Society championship with this Colby. Mild and smooth with a good mouth feel, this is real Colby, not the mild cheddars that masquerade for this Wisconsin original. Slightly tangy and subtle, this is a good munching cheese.

BLUES

Tony and Julie Hook made not just one, but four fabulous blue cheeses, and I can't mention one without mentioning the others. The Gorgonzola is sharp with an underlying sweetness and a distinctive tang. The Tilston Point is an English-style blue that is salty yet smooth and creamy, with layer upon layer of flavor. Smooth and less sharp, Blue Paradise is a double cream blue, and though it's

milder, it still has a distinctive tang. Hook's Blue is salty and creamy, and by far, it's the strongest of the bunch.

AGED CHEDDARS

When I first tasted their cheddars, I was in the company of a New York City chef. This chef let out an audible sigh after he bit into the 10-year-old aged cheddar. "This is what cheddar is supposed to taste like," he said. I couldn't agree more. Whether it is the 5-, 7-, or 10-year-old aged cheddar, they're all delightful. Personally, though, I'm with the

There's always a crowd at Tony and Julie Hook's stand at the Dane County Farmer's Market.

chef—I love the 10-year-old. Intense and extremely sharp, this cheddar's flavor lingers in your mouth, finishing with a salty sweetness. My husband, Kyle, however, prefers the seven-year-old cheddar, which offers a strong, but not too strong, cheddar flavor and a sharpness that isn't too sharp.

BRUNKOW CHEESE OF WISCONSIN

RAW CHEDDAR SPREAD

This stuff is addictive. Though I generally prefer straight cheese to a spread of any sort, this spread is sweet, sharp, and ooh is it good. It's creamy, but with a distinct bite. It's the kind of spread that actually tastes like real cheese (because, in this case, that's what it is). If you want a quick snack, something to spread on crackers or toast, this is one of the best spreads around.

AVONDALE TRUCKLE

When Brunkow decided to deviate from their 100-plus years of cheddar making, they decided to go into some strong, cellar-aged English varieties. Made from raw milk, Avondale Truckle is one of them. This strong, clothbound cheddar cheese offers a pleasant yet very earthy flavor. Underneath its clothbound rind, it boasts a rich, cream color and a firm texture.

ARGYLSHIRE

This is another of the clothbound cheeses that Brunkow markets under the Fayette Creamery label. Strong, cellar aged, and quite earthy, this raw milk isn't your typical cheese. It's not for the faint of palate, but definitely for connoisseurs who like big flavors.

LITTLE DARLING

This strong flavored, American original comes from pasteurized milk; it's inspired by English farmhouse cheeses and named after

Cheese samples are always popular at the Dane County Farmer's Market.

Darlington, Wisconsin, where it is created. Crafted into small wheels, its complex flavors come from wild molds formed during its cellar aging. Grassy, earthy, and full of bite, it's a mouthful

CHALET CHEESE COOPERATIVE
LIMBURGER
If you've ever seen a foil-wrapped package of Limburger on a grocery store shelf,

Myron Olson and his cadre of cheesemakers are the ones who crafted it. Once upon a time, Limburger enjoyed a kind of aromatic popularity. In fact, the U.S. government used to issue special Limburger licenses (to keep the Swiss cheese manufacturers from flooding the market with too much Limburger during their off-seasons). Limburger fell out of fashion, and Myron is the only cheesemaker in the country who makes it today. Plainly put, Limburger is a stinky cheese, but its bark is worse than its mellow bite. In actuality, Limburger is a delicious washed rind cheese. Any fan of stinky, bandage-wrapped cheeses and washed rind cheeses will consider Limburger to be a

Baby Swiss ages in Chalet Cheese Cooperative

mild delicacy. It's a great cheese, and it is especially good when served on thick, dark rye bread, topped with red onions, perhaps some braunschweiger (liver sausage), and served with a side of spicy honey mustard and a beer. It's a heavenly sandwich.

BABY SWISS

Myron Olson's baby Swiss is sort of the opposite of his Limburger. This award-winning cheese is a mild, gentle Swiss. It offers a subtle flavor and a firm texture; it goes down easily, and after you have one piece, you'll crave a second and then a third. It's a delicious snack cheese, and it's also quite tasty on sandwiches, too.

ROTH KÄSE

GRAND CRU GRUYÈRE

This Swiss family-owned cheese company makes a lot of different specialty cheeses, but their signature cheese is Gruyère. This delicious Gruyère isn't made in the Alpine pastures of

Roth Käse workers press cheese curds into molds

Switzerland, but you'll think it was. With nutty and fruity undertones, it tastes great with a glass of wine or used in a fondue. This award-winning cheese comes in three different ages. The basic is aged and washed for four months, the reserve is aged for a minimum of six months, and the surchoix is aged for nine months and longer.

GRANQUESO

Inspired by the great Manchegos of Spain, GranQueso is another award-winner, offering distinct layers of flavor. But unlike the cheeses it pays homage to, this cheese is made with cow's milk instead of sheep's

Cheese curds fill molds at Roth Käse

by raw milk, Alpine-style cheese, but if you can manage to get your hands on this special washed rind, you'll definitely enjoy it. Layer upon layer of flavor explodes in your mouth. This is a cheese with some depth. Earthy and almost barny, it has oomph to spare.

KRÖNENOST FONTINA

This isn't an Italian-style melting cheese; instead, it's inspired by the Swedish version. Krönenost Fontina offers a salty sweet flavor, but it's not overpowering. It's different from most fontinas out there, and it's worth a try. It's a great fondue cheese, too.

milk. Aged for a minimum of six months, it offers a bit of a bite and a pleasant finish.

BUTTERMILK BLUE

This creamy blue has a tasty bite to it. Made from the raw milk of, primarily, Jersey cows, this strong cheese is decadent, tangy, and bright blue in color. I like spooning it into my mouth straight, but my husband requires a cracker to finish it.

ROTH'S PRIVATE RESERVE

This cheese was just barely edged out of first place at the 2007 U.S. Cheese Championship to take first runner-up. It's a hard to come

CARR VALLEY CHEESE

APPLEWOOD SMOKED CHEDDAR

Sid Cook makes so many unusual cheeses, it's easy to forget that he started with cow's milk cheddar. He does, in fact, make about 15 different cheddars, from baby fresh cheddar to big old 74-pound wheels. My

favorite, though, is his applewood smoked cheddar. This white cheddar is smoked with applewood, then rubbed with paprika. Its distinctively smoky flavor is more than slightly addictive.

CREAMA KASA
This triple crème cheese is made in 5-pound wheels. Buttery in flavor and texture, it spreads easily over crusty French bread. Rich and flavorful, it's an easy cheese for eating.

BELGIOIOSO CHEESE
AMERICAN GRANA
If you like Parmesan, you'll love this award-winning, 18-month aged variety that Errico Auricchio specializes in. This reserve Parmesan offers a nutty, sweet flavor, with layers of nuance and taste. Though it's wonderful shaved over pasta, it tastes absolutely divine when drizzled with an aged balsamic vinegar.

AGED PROVOLONE
BelGioioso makes five different types of provolone, and this is my favorite. There's a rich depth to this semisoft cheese. It's piquant yet not overpowering. Made from whole milk, it is aged from five months to up to a year, and it's perfect for snacking.

MONTFORTE-WISCONSIN FARMER'S UNION SPECIALTY CHEESE
MONTFORTE BLUE AND MONTFORTE GORGONZOLA
This little cheese factory makes only two types of cheese—blue and Gorgonzola—but they do make them exceptionally well. Though they've only been making cheese since 2002, their cheeses won first places in the American Cheese Society and World Cheese Championship in 2006. The blue is a good, all-around blue. Firmly textured, it's not too overpowering, not too strong, yet definitely tasty. The Gorgonzola is a bit on the spicy side, with a creamier texture and nice full body. It's easy to see why these cheeses have won the awards they have.

BASS LAKE CHEESE FACTORY

BUTTER JACK WITH CINNAMON

This is perhaps the perfect breakfast cheese. Toast some raisin bread, then add a slice of butter jack with cinnamon and drizzle with just a bit of honey. Mmm . . . this buttery, firm cheese is sweet, but not too sweet, and the cinnamon really accents the cheese's natural aromas and flavors.

TRUFFLE JACK

You want umami flavor, you got it in this strong, aromatic cheese. Black truffles play a starring role in this creamy yet firm cheese. The truffle aroma fills your mouth with

Fresh chilies like these at the Dane County Farmer's Market sometimes flavor cheeses

even the tiniest bite. This cheese is especially good with scrambled eggs drizzled with truffle oil.

FOUR-YEAR-OLD CHEDDAR, MERLOT CHEDDAR

The four-year-old cheddar boasts a nice tang to it, with the right amount of bite. It has a lot of flavor, but it is not too overpowering. The same could be said of the merlot cheddar—a lot of flavor, but not too much. The merlot version is a mild cheddar that boasts a delicate red veining from the wine. The wine's berry aromas marry nicely with the cheddar's delicious tang.

BLASER'S USA INC.

ANTONELLA FORMAGGIO

The Antonella Formaggio line of cheeses by Blaser's is an overall nice and savory bunch of cheeses. There are eight flavors of formaggio: capers & black peppercorns, scallions & crushed rosemary, garden vegetable & sweet basil, olive pimento & lemon pepper, pepperoni & marinara, jalapeño peppers, garlic chive & spring dill, and roasted garlic & tomato basil. What each flavor of formaggio has in common is the sweet, soft, mellow and almost Muenster-provolone–like base of cheese. They are attractive cheeses, with the wheels and half-wheels completely coated in the herbs. As such, these Italian-inspired cheeses really allow the herbs and spices to shine. When you bite into a piece of the scallions & crushed rosemary, the aroma of the fresh herbs fills your mouth and tingles your tongue. When you taste the garlic chive & spring dill, the fragrance of the dill almost tickles your nose—it is that fresh.

BLASER'S MUENSTER AND CRANBERRY MUENSTER

American Muenster cheese isn't at all like its aromatic European counterparts, but I have a soft spot for this cheese since it was my favorite cheese as a child, and I loved snacking on pieces of this white cheese with the annatto rind in between pieces of crisp apples. Blaser's is a very mild, sweet Muenster, and the dried cranberries really accent the cheese's inherent sweetness. The cranberry especially is a good snacking cheese. Also worth trying is Blaser's Caraway Swedish Brick, which is more like a mild cheddar than a brick, but the caraway seeds add a spicy-sweetness that makes this cheese perfect for grilled cheese on rye sandwiches.

CASTLEROCK ORGANIC DAIRY

CASTLEROCK BLUE

Some connoisseurs compare Castlerock with Maytag, but I think Castlerock is in a category all its own. This is a tangy, rich blue cheese, and it's got bite, but it's not too sharp. It's a smooth, almost mellow blue cheese, and there's a layer of depth. You can really taste the milk in this cheese. It's not too salty, not too sharp, but definitely blue and definitely good.

HARVEST MOON

Castlerock makes a cheddarlike cheese they call Harvest Moon. It's sweet, young, and almost melts on your tongue. Like Castlerock's blue, you can really taste the organic milk in this cheese. There's a little, subtle tang to this firm cheese.

LoveTree Farmstead Cheese

Gabrielson Lake

Mary Falk may specialize in sheep's milk cheeses, but she also makes a stunning raw cow's milk cheese, and Gabrielson Lake is it. Created from a single herd of Jersey dairy cows, this cheese has a buttery taste with nutty tones and a fruit finish. It's quite good.

Holland's Family Farm

Marieke Gouda

Cheesemaker Marieke Penterman and her husband, Rolf, hungered for the real, aged Goudas that they had left behind in the Netherlands when they moved to Wisconsin to start their dairy farm. So Marieke returned to the Netherlands to study at a farmhouse Gouda-maker, and since she's returned, she's been making the real thing. Unlike most American or imported Dutch Goudas, the Goudas the Dutch eat in the Netherlands are aged. Her aged, raw milk

Gouda is one of the best Goudas I've ever had the pleasure of tasting. It has a sweet, milky aroma, and a really sweet—almost honeylike—taste. It is an amazing cheese with layers of flavor. The young and pasteurized versions are also good, but the raw milk, aged version is the best.

Marieke Gouda, Flavored Goudas

All of her spices are imported from the Netherlands, and they form the base for her flavored line of Goudas. She makes a dozen different flavors, including cumin, yellow mustard, black mustard, melange mustard, burning melange, burning nettle, onion and garlic, Italian herb, smoked, garden herb, foenugreek, and black pepper. Especially good is her foenugreek, which is a seed that has a sweet, maple syrup–like taste. It's easy to understand why it won first in its class at the 2007 U.S. Cheese Championships, as the sweet spice brings out the sweet tanginess of the cheese; the flavor is subtle, but there's a lot of it to go around. Also quite good and rather unusual is the cumin, which brings out different nuances in the cheese than the foenugreek does; the cumin is spicier and more savory. The mustard flavored cheeses are also savory, but the mustard seeds do not overpower the cheese, and in the Italian spice, you can really taste the spices.

SAXON CREAMERY
MOUNTAIN AND TRAPPIST STYLE CHEESES

More than 10 years in the making, the Saxon Creamery just started aging their first cheeses at the end of summer 2007. They make seven raw milk, pasture-grazed cheeses, all of which are American originals. The cheeses include Green Fields, a washed rind aged for a minimum of 60 days; Saxony, a firm, washed rind with a nutty flavor; Pastures, a firm cheese aged for a minimum of 90 days; Big Ed's, a cooked curd, firm cheese aged for a minimum of 240 days; Meadows, which are carefully selected wheels of Pastures aged for 275 days; Stone Silo, a sweet natural rind; and Grandpa Ed's, like Big Ed's but aged for a year or more.

CHAPTER 8

The Artisanal and Specialty
GOAT AND SHEEP CHEESES

FANTÔME FARM
FRESH AND FLEURIE NOIR GOAT CHEESES

Goat cheese doesn't get any better than this. Anne Topham, one of the very first farmstead goat cheesemakers in the United States, makes a bounty of both fresh and aged goat cheeses. Her fresh, melt-on-your-tongue cheeses come in plain or with the addition of herbs. Her garlic chèvre is creamy, savory, and really fresh. She also serves the fresh goat cheese marinated in extra virgin olive oil. It is also formed into logs with dried thyme. Although her cheese is wonderful fresh, the Fleurie Noir, a bloomy-rind, aged cheese is even more exceptional. This French-inspired goat cheese, is dusted with ash and salt, then aged for several weeks. Her cheese is only available from April until December.

CAPRINE SUPREME
FRESH CHÈVRE/GOAT'S MILK
CHEESE SPREADS

Todd Jaskolski just started making fresh chèvre in 2007, but with the quality of milk his wife, Sheryl, coaxes from their herd, it's a natural fit. This chèvre is very mild, sweet, and tangy. Todd mixes in different herbs and bacon, and the bacon spread is exceptionally savory.

DREAMFARM
FRESH GOAT CHEESE

The computerization of graphic arts and a few pet goats convinced Diana Murphy to make goat cheese. Her small herd makes such high-quality milk that it's easy to see how Diana's developed such a following at the West Side Market in Madison. Her chèvre comes plain, mixed with herbs, or presented in olive oil. Sweet, tangy, and fresh, her chèvre is just delightful.

BASS LAKE CHEESE FACTORY
CANASTA PARDO

Made in baskets, this firm sheep's milk cheese is hand-rubbed with cinnamon.

Diana Murphy doesn't milk her goats in winter, but she still has fun with them.

The sweet richness of the sheep's milk is accented by the spicy tang of the cinnamon. It's a glorious, delicious cheese with a depth of flavor and nuance. Cheesemaker Scott Erickson makes more than 50 different cheeses, but this is my favorite of his, hands down.

GOAT MUENSTER WITH GREEN OLIVES

This mildly sweet, firm cheese is delicious. The olives really bring out the natural tang of the goat's milk, and the flavors of the two marry well.

CHÈVRE, CHILI PEPPER CHÈVRE

Cheesemaker Scott Erickson makes a good, tangy fresh chèvre, but his chili pepper–infused chèvre is absolutely delightful. The spicy chili peppers give a little more bite, but not too much bite, along with subtle flavors of onion, garlic, and cilantro. It's a tasty cheese that would be an excellent addition to quesadillas or rolled tortillas.

CAPRI CHEESERY

GOAT'S FETAS

Cheesemaker Felix Thalhammer knows his way around feta. In fact, he makes two varieties, Greek and French style. The Greek feta has a strong tang—almost a *kapow* of flavor—you can tell that it's been aged and well cared for. And it's not too salty. The French feta is milder, not as crumbly, with very subtle aromas. It's very good, too. Felix also makes some feta cheese spreads flavored with garlic and dill, basil and tomato, and other herbs and vegetables.

WASHED RIND GOAT'S MILK CHEESES

Felix also makes some goat's milk versions of Muenster cheeses, and these are the authentic, real washed rind kind of Muensters. Highly aromatic, these Washed Bear and Smoky Bear cheeses are mild yet filled with taste. Also quite good are his washed rind Govarti—a cross between Gouda and Havarti—and St. Felix. Beautiful, nutty, and full-flavored, these are all good cheeses.

Brenda Jensen's lambs pose for a picture

HIDDEN SPRINGS CREAMERY

DRIFTLESS CHEESE

Brenda Jensen tends her sheep with great care, and it shows. Her sheep are tended the old-fashioned way, and indeed, her entire farm is run with draft horsepower and no tractors or heavy equipment. This sustainable and all-natural farm creates the perfect setting for amazing cheese. Her sweet, creamy, almost velvety cheeses with just a smidgen of tang practically melt on your tongue and explode with flavor. It would seem that Brenda has been practicing organic farming and cheese-making for years, but her cheeses are one of the newest artisanal dairy products in the state, having just become available to consumers in the spring of 2006. Though a newbie, Brenda practically swept the fresh sheep's milk cheese category of the 2007 U.S. Cheese Championship, with her lavender and honey taking top honors, followed by plain in second place, and basil taking fourth. Regular offerings include plain, the candylike lavender and honey, and the savory basil. In the fall, Brenda also crafts pumpkin, gingerbread spice, and cranberry versions, She just began aging her cheeses, which I expect to be divine.

MT. STERLING CHEESE COOPERATIVE

FLAVORED FRESH JACKS

This award-winning Monterey Jack–style cheese comes plain or in six flavors: dill, garlic, onion, chives, jalapeño peppers, or tomato & basil. Mild and extremely moist, these cheeses offer a gentle tang of flavor without being overpowering. Similar to a jack made with cow's milk, this semisoft cheese is meltable and great tossed in salads.

RAW MILK CHEDDAR

Unpasteurized and as natural as can be, this is the cheese that built the Mt. Sterling

Cheese Cooperative. As perhaps the only cheddar made with raw goat's milk in the country, this tasty cheddar holds a soft yet firm texture with a slight sense of saltiness. Milder than most cow's milk cheddars, this cheese still has that distinctive flavor you expect from a cheddar. Aged for 60 days, it offers a slightly nutty yet very balanced taste. They make an aged, an organic, and a no-salt version, too.

LOVETREE FARMSTEAD CHEESE

TRADE LAKE CEDAR

Trade Lake Cedar is one of those unforgettable cheeses. Aged on boughs of cedar in Mary and David Falk's cave, this raw sheep's milk cheese has a complex flavor . . . Mary likens it to a walk in the North Woods. Undertones of fruit and wood mingle; it's quite magical, especially served with a crusty, cinnamon raisin baguette and a glass of syrah or red zinfandel.

FISH BAIT

These are the younger sheep's milk cheeses that Mary makes. Aged only between four and six weeks, they are rolled in charcoal or herbs. For those who have had the pleasure of tasting them, they are just a bit of nirvana. Also, they are sold as "fish bait" because they are made from raw milk and not aged 60 days. Although I'm sure perch or bass would appreciate them, I think you'll enjoy them more.

MONTCHEVRÉ-BETIN

FRESH CHÈVRE

It's easy to think you're in France after biting into a bit of Montchevré-Betin's fresh goat chèvre. Cheesemaker Jean Rossard cut his

teeth in making fresh goat chèvre pyramides in France, and his French culinary background shines through in every log of cheese. Though he doesn't make everything by hand like he did when he first started making cheese, the same fine attention to detail and quality comes through. Sweet, tangy, and unmistakably chèvre, this fresh cheese is good tossed in pasta, served hot over a salad of mixed greens, or just by itself. The range of flavors offered includes lemon zest, sun-dried tomato, garlic & herbs, and four pepper, with my personal favorite being four pepper. Jean also makes a mean goat milk Camembert and a tasty aged bucheron.

CARR VALLEY CHEESE

COCOA CARDONA

While Sid Cook's mixed milks take most of the attention, he also makes 10 different purely goat's milk cheeses. Aged and rubbed with dark cocoa and just a little black pepper, this fantastic cheese is semisoft, with more than a hint of sweetness and a bit of a spicy bite. It won best of its class in the 2003 American Cheese Society competition. It's a great cheese to serve with French bread or croissants, and it pairs up perfectly with port.

CHAPTER 9

The Artisanal and Specialty
MIXED MILK
CHEESES

CARR VALLEY CHEESE

Fourth generation cheesemaker Sid Cook knows his way around a creamery. So well that he is considered by many to be the most decorated cheesemaker in America, and his American originals have earned more than 100 top national and international awards. His company makes more than 75 different cheeses in all, and Sid is always experimenting and coming up with new cheeses all the time, especially those made from mixed milks.

BESSIE'S BLEND

Cook originally intended to call this mixed milk cheese "50-50" because it is made with equal parts cow and goat milks. "We told him that was too unexciting," says Patty Aoenig, who works at Carr Valley. So Sid decided to name it after his long-term secretary, who also happens to be Aoenig's mom. "If you work here long enough, you'll get a cheese named after you, provided you have the right sort of name," Aoenig laughs, and then adds that she's still waiting to have one named after

Menage, Shepherd's Blend, Grand Canaria, and Mellage are just some of the mixed milk cheeses Sid Cook crafts by hand.

herself. But instead of waiting for Patty's Cheese, do try Bessie's. This nutty and slightly salty cheese boasts a burst of flavor.

GRAN CANARIA

This is the cheese that put Sid and Carr Valley Cheese on the map. It won Best of Show at the 2004 American Cheese Society competition, and with good reason. This triple milk cheese is aged at least two years and cured in olive oil. Nutty, sweet, and utterly decadent, it's easy to see why it became the first mixed milk cheese to ever take top honors in the competition.

K & K CHEESE / NATURAL VALLEY CHEESE

COW BILLY

This washed rind, cave-aged cheese is a wonder to behold—and to taste. Earthy and pungent yet not overpowering, this cheese offers depth. Cheesemaker Tom Torkelson

gets all of his milk from Amish farmers, and it's as close to organic as possible without having the label (only 12 percent of his farmers have actually gone to the trouble of getting certified). Nutty yet earthy, with a subtle bit of goat tang, this cheese, which took second place at the 2007 American Cheese Society competition, has layers of depth and tons of flavor. Not only is it delicious, but it has one of the most playful names of any American original cheese.

CAPRI CHEESERY

ST. PAULINE

Cheesemaker Felix Thalhammer knows his way around goat's milk cheeses, and this washed rind is a blend of goat's milk and cow's milk. The tang of goat is balanced by the more mellow cow's milk. It has a depth of flavor and lots of nuance—at times, it almost tastes herbal because the animals whose milk is used are all grass-fed.

CHAPTER 10

Other Artisanal
DAIRY
PRODUCTS
(Including Yogurt, Ice Cream, Butter, and Milk)

BLUE MARBLE DAIRY

MILK, CREAM, SMOOTHIES

Nick Kirch's milk, cream, and smoothies are some of the best milks around. Naturally sweet, they're not homogenized (but are pasteurized), and they're incredible for not only drinking but also cooking; his cream makes the most velvety sauces and desserts. His chocolate milk, which needs to be shaken, isn't overly sweet, and it's unlike anything else you'd find on supermarket shelves. His fruit smoothies are recently developed and come in a variety of flavors.

CAPRINE SUPREME

GOAT'S MILK YOGURT

Todd Jaskolski started with yogurt, and his delicious, sweet, and tangy blended yogurt is *so* good. Because of the nature of goat's milk and the process of yogurt making, it's a little thinner yogurt than the cow's milk varieties (cow's milk yogurt is often bulked up with dried milk powder, and there isn't much dried goat's milk powder available). It's texture, though, is creamy and satiny, and the flavor is sweetly delightful. Try it plain, or flavored with vanilla, peach, blueberry, or strawberry.

CRYSTAL BALL FARMS

MILK, CREAM, BUTTER, SMOOTHIES, ICE CREAM

Troy and Barb DeRosier's farm is all organic, and that rich, natural sweetness comes out in the milk. Their milks and creams are sweet, rich, and nonhomogenized. The same can be said for their butter and ice cream. The ice cream is especially good, and it comes in several fruit flavors: strawberry, buttermilk blueberry, peach, and banana, along with chocolate, chocolate mint, and chocolate peanut butter. And they've just introduced a line of smoothies, which are also quite good.

CASTLEROCK ORGANIC DAIRY

MILK, CREAM, ICE CREAM

Organic, sweet, and nonhomogenized, this milk is exceptionally good. But even better are the ice creams: chocolate molasses, cookies 'n cream, pumpkin spice, chocolate mint, and almost a dozen other flavors. Sweet, but not too sweet, the ice cream is rich and buttery.

DAVIS FARM
MILK, CREAM

All natural, nothing but the good stuff: That's what milk and cream at Judy and John Davis's farmstead dairy tastes like. It's probably the smallest farmstead dairy in the state, and their milk and cream are amazingly fresh. The chocolate milk especially is addictive.

MT. STERLING CHEESE COOPERATIVE
WHEY CREAM GOAT BUTTER

One of the only butters made with goat's milk instead of cow's milk, this lightly salted butter boasts a pure, chalky white color and a sweet creaminess. Rich and flavorful, it has an almost silky texture, and it has more sweetness than the typical cow's milk butter. Delicious on biscuits and crusty bread, it's great for cooking, and it's not just for those who suffer from allergies to cow's milk.

SIBBY'S ORGANIC ICE CREAM
ICE CREAM

Though Sibby doesn't make 31 flavors, her vanilla and chocolate are good enough to boast about. Her vanilla, in particular, is one of the sweetest, best tasting vanilla ice creams around, and it is perfect for ice cream sundaes.

SUGAR RIVER YOGURT
PLAIN AND FLAVORED YOGURTS

One of the richest, best tasting yogurts around, it's hard to believe it's low-fat. The unhomogenized milk makes a difference— it's so creamy and naturally sweet. Yogurts come in vanilla, plain, and several fruit flavors. My favorite is plain, mixed with fresh berries.

TETZNER DAIRY
MILK, CREAM, ICE CREAM, ICE CREAM SANDWICHES

Phillip Tetzner and his son and grandsons bottle milk and make ice cream right on the farm. The fresh, natural milk is bottled in plastic bags, and it's fresh and good. But the ice cream is really wonderful. Cherry nut, chocolate mint, and peppermint are some of the flavors. What tastes even better than the ice cream are the homemade ice cream sandwiches, which are made right on the farm. At only a dollar apiece, they're quite a sweet bargain. They're also worth the drive all the way up to Lake Superior.

WEBER DAIRY

MILK, CREAM, EGGNOG

Fresh and delicious, Weber Dairy milk is bottled right on the farm in plastic pouches. Their chocolate milk is quite good, and during the holidays they also make a reduced-fat eggnog. They also offer what is perhaps the only drive-through farmstead dairy in the country, so it's worth a visit. While you're driving through, you can pick up some cheese, eggs, meat, and even fish bait, but what's also quite good are their homemade ice cream pies and sundaes.

Phillip Tetzner's goats are just pets.

These kitties hang out in an Amish barn.

CHAPTER 11

The Future of
WISCONSIN
CHEESE

WISCONSIN HAS BEEN KNOWN AS AMERICA'S DAIRYLAND FOR longer than most people can remember, but it's been more than a decade since California exceeded Wisconsin in overall milk production, and many prognosticators say that any day now, California will exceed Wisconsin in cheese production, too. Or not—it depends on whom you talk to. But even if California takes away Wisconsin's commodity cheese mantle, cheese isn't going away in the least.

In fact, cheese production continues to grow in Wisconsin, but unlike the western states that produce cheese, it isn't the big business that's growing. Artisanal cheesemakers continue to pop up, sometimes on a monthly basis, and the specialty cheese business is booming. Though Wisconsin's dairy infrastructure tended to favor larger plants at one time, in recent years it has become much more balanced, and one of the big equalizers was the Dairy Business Innovation Center (DBIC).

The formation of the Dairy Business Innovation Center in 2004 has really aided new cheesemakers and artisanal dairy producers. The center's main purpose is to help the little guys get their businesses going. Someone who makes great goat's milk feta, for example, might not have the connections to get their cheese placed in specialty grocery stores. Someone who makes organic blue cheese might not know how to design an eye-catching label. "Our whole goal is to do one-on-one consulting with anyone who's interested or who wants to get involved in the industry, to help them through all the rules and regulations, finally through to the marketing and the profitability," says Dan Carter, founder and chairman of the DBIC.

Half of the center's operating budget goes out as grants to cheese and dairy entrepreneurs. It has sent cheesemakers out to the National Association for the Specialty Food Trade (NASFT) Fancy Foods show, and it's also sent them to Europe to study and research different aspects of cheesemaking. But one of the biggest things it does is connect cheesemakers, yogurt makers, and milk bottlers with experts who can get them the know-how they need to succeed in their small businesses. "I love these little people," says Neville McNaughton, a technical consultant for the DBIC who originally was a cheesemaker in New Zealand. "They're the people with the least resources and the most questions. It's hard to put a value on answering a question for a cheesemaker, but it's huge. Within the larger dairy and cheese companies, they have most of the questions answered, but they're extremely good at keeping those answers within those companies."

Demystifying what works and what doesn't helps, and so does simple exposure. One other thing Wisconsin's little (and sometimes big) cheese-

Each one of these wheels weighs about 200 pounds.

makers have done is to do their job well, and then win awards that show it. Almost every year, the U.S. Cheese Championships and the American Cheese Society competition are dominated by Wisconsin cheeses. Sometimes, these wins are expected—Sid Cook, for four years running, has walked away with record-breaking numbers of ribbons at the ACS; taking home 28 awards, including 8 first-place ribbons in 2007. Some are newbies like Marieke Penterman, whose foenugreek Gouda took first place in the flavored semisoft cheese category at the 2007 U.S. Cheese Championship, less than six months after she started making cheese. And sometimes these wins are the first-ever or incredibly notable American wins at international cheese competitions, when Wisconsin cheeses knock out their European competitors, like when Montforte's Gorgonzola took first place at the World Cheese Championships in London.

Some of the winners at these big competitions are big dairy, and some of Wisconsin's big dairies are starting to get into the specialty game, either by actually devoting part of their cheese production to smaller, original batches, or just by marketing themselves as artisans. The marketing ploys are a bit scary, and it's not just Wisconsin's bigger companies that are doing it—other national cheese companies are also getting into the game. Fortunately, actual quality tends to speak for itself, and if consumers like what the big guys are doing, perhaps they'll be led into the even more amazing creations of the little guys, too. At least that is my fervent hope.

It's also my desire that other people fall in love with Wisconsin cheese. It's easy to do once you taste it, and for me, living in Milwaukee means that I have access to a lot of Wisconsin's great cheeses. If you don't live in my fine state, plenty of its cheese makes its way to other states (and even countries), and sometimes, you can even see it on television. The History Channel did a show in 2007, *Modern Marvels: Cheese,* which featured several Wisconsin cheesemakers. In 2008, Wisconsin will be featured, this time in an international show, "Cheese Slices," a show that airs on Australia's version of the Food Network.

Wisconsin cheese also, not surprisingly, shows up on the Web. One of the cutest Wisconsin cheese Web sites was created by a group of Wauwatosa, Wisconsin, students at

Some cheeses like Gruyère are brined before aging.

Roosevelt Elementary School (http://library.thinkquest.org/5417), but one of the most informative—and actually one of my personal favorites—is a Wisconsin cheese blog, Madison writer Jeanne Carpenter's www.cheeseunderground.blogspot.com. Jeanne, who used to work for the DBIC, is dialed into the latest happenings in the Wisconsin cheese world, and just about every week, or at least, every month, there's either a new cheesemaker getting ready to rock and roll, or an existing cheesemaker unveiling an exciting new product. She invites visitors with the line, "Welcome to Wisconsin, the Dairy Artisan Mecca of the World."

I couldn't have said it better. And, as I write this, I've learned of yet another new artisanal cheese plant that's making cheese. It couldn't be a more exciting time to live in Wisconsin if you love cheese. And even if you don't live in Wisconsin, if you love cheese, it's exciting to see where these new cheesemakers are going.

Visiting the CHEESEMAKERS

CHAPTER 12

The CHEESEMAKERS *Who Invite Visitors*

MOST OF THE CHEESEMAKERS AND ARTISANAL DAIRY FOLK IN Wisconsin not only accept visitors, but even delight in having their customers come out to see them. Many of the cheesemakers or milk bottlers or ice cream makers have little stores on their farms or at their cheese factories, and visitors can drop in anytime. Others do not have formal stores, but they do accept visitors at their farms if people call ahead of time.

DROP-IN VISITS

BASS LAKE CHEESE FACTORY

598 Valley View Trail
Somerset, WI 54025
800-368-2437
www.blcheese.com

HOURS: 10–6, Monday through Saturday.
Closed on Sunday and holidays.

DESCRIPTION: Not only does this small factory sell its cheese through a charming store, but visitors can also watch cheese being made through a viewing window. Cheesemaker Scott Erickson also has one of the best collections of antique cheesemaking, dairy, and farm equipment around, which is displayed in the shop. Every Saturday they also host a wine and cheese tasting for customers.

BLASER'S USA INC.

(SIGN SAYS MAMA CURELLA)
1858 Highway 63
Comstock, WI 54826
715- 822-2437
www.blasersusa.com

HOURS: 9–5, Monday through Saturday; 10–5, Sunday.

DESCRIPTION: This little Northwestern cheese factory store is the only one with a decidedly Italian flavor. Blaser's artisanal Antonella line of cheeses is featured, and the store also has a real Italian deli with paninis, salads, and imported Tuscan wines. They make their own fudge, too, and there's a pastoral picnic area

Even though they weigh about 200 pounds, the salt in the brine causes these wheels of Swiss to float.

outside. Visitors can also watch cheesemaking from windows outside the little factory. In front of the old cheesemaker's quarters is a gorgeous flower pot; the pot is actually one of the original copper vats that was used to make Swiss cheese.

BRUNKOW CHEESE OF WISCONSIN

17975 County Highway F
Darlington, WI 53530
800-338-3773
www.pcmli.com/cw_bk.htm

HOURS: 8–3, Monday to Friday; 8–1, Saturday; and 8–noon, Sunday.

DESCRIPTION: This small, historic cheese plant

has a small store, and if it's not too busy, they might even be able to take you in back to see the cheesemaking operations (but call ahead to confirm). They also sell their cheese during the summer months at numerous farmer's markets, including Madison's Dane County Farmer's Market, and some in Chicago farmer's markets.

CARR VALLEY CHEESE

S3797 County Trunk Highway G
LaValle, WI 53941
608-986-2781
www.carrvalleycheese.com

HOURS: 8–4, Monday through Saturday; closed Sunday.

DESCRIPTION: Carr Valley has a couple different cheese plants and retail store locations (visit their Web site for more details), but this little store also has a little something extra: a professional cooking school. The school offers not only cheese classes, but it also brings in chefs from across the country who use Carr Valley cheese in their cooking.

CASTLE ROCK ORGANIC DAIRY

S13240 Young Road
Osseo, WI 54758
715-597-0085
www.castlerockfarms.net

HOURS: 8–8, daily.

DESCRIPTION: This organic dairy and cheese-making factory sells its own organic milk, cheese, ice cream, and butter, along with organic meats. There is a viewing window so

you can see the milk being bottled or the cheese being made. Once a year they host a customer appreciation day, and tours are given of their small plant.

CEDAR GROVE CHEESE

E5904 Mill Road
Plain, WI 53577
800-200-6020
www.cedargrovecheese.com

HOURS: 8–4:30, Monday through Saturday; 9–1, Sunday.

DESCRIPTION: Not only is there a viewing window for visitors to see the organic cheese being made, but visitors can also tour their Living Machine to see how they naturally treat wastewater using microbes, plants, and little snails.

CHALET CHEESE COOPERATIVE

N4858 County N
Monroe, WI 53566
608-325-4343

HOURS: 7–3:30, Monday through Friday; 8–10, Saturday; closed Sunday.

DESCRIPTION: Though they don't let visitors wander in the cheese factory, visitors can still see Limburger being wrapped in foil by hand, and packaged.

CRYSTAL BALL FARMS

527 State Road 35
Osceola, WI 54020

HOURS: 8–6, Monday through Friday; 8–noon, Saturday; closed Sunday.

DESCRIPTION: This little organic dairy bottles its own milk, makes its own ice cream and smoothies, and even makes some cheese curds. Its bucolic little store sits right on the farm, and visitors can sometimes see the cows, but they can always see the milk being bottled through the viewing window—it's bottled fresh every day. Once a year, Troy and Barb DeRosier host a free Special Kids' Day for children with special needs and their families.

DAVIS FARM

North 5026 County J
Kennan, WI 54537
715-474-3454

HOURS: Open every day, self-service, but call ahead on holidays.

At Hidden Springs Creamery, the sheep roam right outside the creamery.

DESCRIPTION: This little family farm bottles its own milk and cream, and it also sells meat, cheese, and vegetables from its on-farm store. Visitors can see the cows, geese, bunnies, and draft horses on this beautiful farm.

HENNING'S WISCONSIN CHEESE

20201 Ucker Point Creek Road
Kiel, WI 53042
920-894-3032
www.henningscheese.com

HOURS: 6–3, Monday through Friday; 8–noon, Saturday; closed Sunday.

DESCRIPTION: It's pretty exciting when master cheesemaker Kerry Henning crafts his mammoth, 12,000-pound wheels of cheddar, but he doesn't make them every day. Visitors to their store, however, can see cheese being made through viewing windows, and they also can view a film to see their spectacular giants.

HOLLAND'S FAMILY FARM

N13851 Gorman Avenue
Thorp, WI 54771
715-669-5230
www.hollandsfamilycheese.com

HOURS: 9–5, Monday through Friday; 10–4, Saturday; closed Sunday.

DESCRIPTION: An unpaved road leads to this authentic Dutch farmstead creamery where Marieke and Rolf Penterman and their family make real Gouda. Their farmstead creamery store has viewing windows of the cheesemaking and aging rooms, and the store also sells Dutch and other European imports. Tours of the farm can be arranged, but they must be scheduled in advance.

HOOK'S CHEESE COMPANY

320 Commerce Street
Mineral Point, WI 53565
608-987-3259

HOURS: 4 AM–3 PM, Friday; sometimes other days, but call ahead.

DESCRIPTION: Husband and wife team Tony and Julie Hook make some absolutely incredible aged cheddars, blue cheeses, and other American originals. They make cheese every Friday. Sometimes you can catch them on other days, but it's not guaranteed, so call ahead. Or, just head to the Dane County Farmer's Market (indoors during cold weather months) in Madison every Saturday to buy their award-winning cheese.

K & K CHEESE/NATURAL VALLEY CHEESE

S510 County Highway D
Cashton, WI 54619
608-654-4480

HOURS: 8–5, Monday through Saturday; closed Sunday.

DESCRIPTION: Master cheesemaker Tom Torkelson handcrafts some amazing cheeses from Amish goat's milk and cow's milk. It's a tiny factory store, and don't be surprised if you see Amish buggies in the neighborhood. They also offer tours if you call in advance, and they will

offer tours of their new affinage rooms, too, which are at a separate (but nearby) location.

MONTFORTE-WFU SPECIALTY CHEESE CO. LLC

303 E. Highway 18
Montfort, WI 53569
608-943-6771
www.wfucheese.com

HOURS: 8–5, Monday through Thursday; 8–6, Friday; 8–4, Saturday; 11–4, Sunday.

DESCRIPTION: This is a small cheese factory that makes internationally award-winning blue and Gorgonzola cheeses. Visitors can see the cheese being made through viewing windows at the factory store. They're also encouraged to visit the popcorn store next door, where flavored popcorn is made from corn grown in the area.

MT. STERLING CHEESE COOPERATIVE

505 Diagonal Street
Mt. Sterling, WI 54645
608-734-3151
www.buygoatcheese.com

HOURS: 8–4, Monday through Friday; closed weekends.

DESCRIPTION: This little cooperative (and we do mean little) actually is one of the country's largest goat's milk cooperatives, and they make some amazing goat's milk cheddars, jacks, and whey cream butter. A viewing window allows visitors to their on-site store to see cheese being made. There are a lot of apple orchards in the area, which are popular during the fall months.

ROTH KÄSE

You can view the cheesemaking process at Roth Käse from an observation deck.

ROTH KÄSE
627 Second Street
Monroe, WI 53566
608-328-3355
www.rothkase.com

HOURS: 9–5, Monday through Saturday; 10–4, Sunday.

DESCRIPTION: This small but highly efficient modern cheese plant has a beautiful little store, and there's an observation deck where visitors can watch Gruyère being aged and brined. Group tours are available by appointment, and this Swiss cheese factory also boasts a modern test kitchen for visiting chefs.

SAXON CREAMERY
855 Hickory Street
Cleveland, WI 53015
920-693-8500
www.saxoncreamery.com

HOURS: noon–6, Wednesday through Saturday.

DESCRIPTION: This farmstead creamery is one of the newest in the state of Wisconsin. Besides making great cheeses, they also are one of the most environmentally friendly farms in the Midwest. Tours are by appointment only.

SIBBY'S ICE CREAM
Viroqua Public Market/Sibby's Organic Zone Ice Cream Parlor
215 South Main Street
Viroqua, WI 54665
608-637-1912
www.sibbysicecream.com

HOURS: 10–5, Tuesday through Friday; 9–5, Saturday; noon–4, Sunday; closed Monday.

DESCRIPTION: Sibby makes some of the best organic ice cream on the planet, and her Organic Zone (OZ for short) Ice Cream Parlor serves up ice cream sundaes, shakes, and other goodies. Sibby (Sue Huber) also accepts visitors at her farmstead ice cream operation: S2987 Sebion Road, Westby, WI 54667, but you should call ahead at 608-634-3828.

TETZNER DAIRY
30455 Nevers Road
Washburn, WI 54891
715-373-2330

HOURS: 6 AM–10 PM, daily.

DESCRIPTION: This little family farmstead dairy bottles milk and makes ice cream from scratch. Especially good are the homemade ice cream sandwiches. The little store is self-service, and cheese, produce, and other Wisconsin goods are also sold. Pet goats and dogs often greet visitors, too, and you'd be hard-pressed to find any other dairy that has a view of Lake Superior.

WEBER DAIRY

9706 County Road H
Marshfield, WI 5449
715-384-5639

HOURS: 8:30–7, Monday through Friday; 8:30–5, Saturday; closed Sunday.

DESCRIPTION: This is probably the only drive-through farmstead dairy store around. Customers drive up to get their farmstead bottled milk and cream, as well as purchase cheese, meat, eggs, juice, and get soft-serve ice cream, ice cream sundaes, and homemade ice cream pies. Visitors can walk into the little store, and they are also invited to visit the calf barn to pet the calves and the kittens.

WIDMER'S CHEESE CELLARS

214 Henni Street
Theresa, WI 53091
888-878-1107
www.widmerscheese.com

HOURS: 6–5, Monday through Friday; 7–4, Saturday. Open 10–4, Sunday, June through October.

DESCRIPTION: Walk in the front door of the cheese factory store, and you're right in the middle of the cheesemaking room. No viewing window separates you from the cheese, and you can see master cheesemaker Joe Widmer and his staff use the same cream city bricks that his grandfather used in the early 1900s. This is also the closest artisanal cheesemaker to the Milwaukee area.

DANE COUNTY FARMER'S MARKET

Capitol Square
Madison, WI
608-455-1999
www.madfarmmkt.org

DESCRIPTION: This is the biggest farmer's market in the country, and here is where you'll find Capri Cheesery, Fantôme Farm, Brunkow Cheese, and Hook's Cheese, plus a couple others. It runs every Saturday; in winter, it moves indoors to the Madison Senior Center, 330 W. Mifflin Street.

CALL-AHEAD VISITS

BLUE MARBLE FAMILY FARM

7571 Kirch Road
Barneveld, WI 53507
608-924-2721
www.bluemarblefamilyfarm.com

DESCRIPTION: This is a small farmstead milk and smoothie bottling operation just outside Madison. Some milk is sold from the farm, but call ahead.

CAPRINE SUPREME

W5646 Highway 54
Black Creek, WI 54106
920-984-3388

DESCRIPTION: This charming goat's milk yogurt and cheese plant is located near Green Bay. It is a farmstead operation, and sometimes you see the goats grazing outside (it's up to the goats whether they graze or not). Owner Todd Jaskolski has plans to set up a more formal store and welcome center with regular hours.

Roth Käse's wheels of cheese are aged for several months.

DREAMFARM

8877 Table Bluff Road
Cross Plains, WI 53528
608-767-3442
www.dreamfarm.biz

DESCRIPTION: Farmstead cheesemaker Diana Murphy handcrafts fresh chèvre from her small herd. She also raises organic chickens and sells their eggs. Most Saturdays she can be found at the West Side (of Madison) Farmer's Market, but she will sell her cheese from her farm if you call ahead. Her goats are extremely friendly, and they love visitors. Every year, she also hosts a farm day for her customers.

EDELWEISS TOWNHALL CREAMERY

W6117 County C
Monticello, WI 53570
608-938-4094

HOURS: Cheese is for sale most mornings, but call ahead.

DESCRIPTION: This is the only place in the United States where you can see big wheel, traditional Emmentaler cheese made in a copper vat that was once used at a Swiss cheesemaking school. Master cheesemaker Bruce Workman works most mornings, and he or his small staff will sell you cheese right from the factory, but do call ahead—they tend to work in the middle of the night, so some days they finish up earlier than others.

Brenda Jensen blends honey and lavender by hand before she mixes them into her cheese.

HIDDEN SPRINGS CREAMERY

S1597 Hanson Road
Westby, WI 54667
608-634-2521

DESCRIPTION: Brenda Jensen loves visitors, but they must call ahead. In fact, she and her husband have recently built a bed & breakfast so visitors can stay on their beautiful farm and creamery.

LOVETREE FARMSTEAD CHEESE

12413 County Road Z
Grantsburg, WI 54840
715-488-2966
www.lovetreefarmstead.com

DESCRIPTION: Mary Falk and her husband, David, make some of the most innovative cheeses in the state, and they operate a completely organic farm, set in the middle of Wisconsin's North Woods. They also have a cave where Mary ages her organic, raw sheep's milk cheeses. Most Saturdays you can find them at the St. Paul Farmer's Market (even in winter . . . they're outside, in snowsuits, selling their cheese). But if you'd like to visit their fantastic farm, do call ahead. They're small, so they need advance warning for guests.

CRAVE BROTHERS FARMSTEAD CHEESE

W11555 Torpy Road
Waterloo, WI 53594
920-478-4887
www.cravecheese.com

DESCRIPTION: The Crave Brothers usually aren't open to the public—they are a small, family-run company, and they don't have enough staff to devote to tours, and at this time they don't have an on-site store. However, every June and July they do host special tours, and they do offer tours by appointment. It's definitely worth a visit, as they have one of the most beautiful test kitchens/tasting rooms for culinary professionals, and their cheese is amazing.

CHAPTER 13

Where to Stay, Where to Eat, and What to See
WHILE VISITING

WISCONSIN ISN'T A SMALL STATE, AND EXCEPT FOR JOE WIDMER, who is about 45 minutes from Milwaukee, and Scott Erickson, who is about 45 minutes from St. Paul, Minnesota, most of the cheesemakers are not located near any large, metropolitan areas. Some, however, are located near smaller cities like Madison, the Eau Claire/Chippewa Valley region, Monroe, Bayfield, Sheboygan, and the Wisconsin Dells.

Most of the cheesemakers are located in some of the most gorgeous Midwestern countryside you could ever see. They're worth a visit, whether you drive in or fly in (to one of the aforementioned cities), but if you fly in, you will need to rent a car to visit them.

Here is a selection of places to stay, eat, and do something interesting while visiting cheesemakers. The travel information is divided into the following sections: Wisconsin Dells/Spring Green and Monroe, for southwest and south central Wisconsin cheesemakers; Eau Claire/Chippewa Valley and Twin Cities, for northwest Wisconsin cheesemakers; Bayfield for Tetzner Dairy (the most northern artisanal dairy); and Sheboygan area for northeastern Wisconsin. This is not a complete listing, but it's a sampling of places you might want to visit when you're traveling to see cheesemakers.

WISCONSIN DELLS / SPRING GREEN

The Wisconsin Dells and Spring Green are two of the most visited Wisconsin tourist destinations. The Dells is known for its water parks and kid-friendly doings while Spring Green is known for a certain Midwestern architect and the House on the Rock.

NORTHERN BAY GOLF RESORT & MARINA

1844 20th Avenue
Arkdale, WI 54613
608-339-2090
www.northernbayresort.com

COST: Summer rates, $149–429, fall/winter, $89–259.

CREDIT CARDS: MasterCard, Visa, Discover, American Express.

DESCRIPTION: Though the Wisconsin Dells is a short drive away, you couldn't be in a more different, more tranquil world than on the banks of Northern Bay. A gorgeous golf course and a marina complement these waterfront condos. The smallest is a large master suite with fireplace and whirlpool, and they go up to four bedrooms.

GREAT WOLF LODGE

1400 Great Wolf Drive
Wisconsin Dells, WI 53965
800-559-WOLF
www.greatwolf.com

COST: $129 and up.

CREDIT CARDS: MasterCard, Visa, American Express, Discover.

DESCRIPTION: Every summer, my mother-in-law, stepfather-in-law, sister-in-law, and nephews Ryan and Eric head here to frolic on the slides, float in the wave pool, and play laser tag and other games. It's one of the country's largest indoor water parks, and it's a great family destination.

BUFFALO PHIL'S GRILLE

150 Gasser Road
Lake Delton, WI 53940
608-254-7300
www.buffalophilsgrille.com

COST: Reasonable.

The American Club serves some of the best Wisconsin cheeses

DESCRIPTION: With indoor video games, race cars, and a bowling alley (all completely non-smoking), this is a fun place to take your kids. It's also well designed and modeled after the old Northern Woods lodges of years past, crafted with real logs from the real Northern Woods. My husband, who is an architect, was particularly impressed with the design. The food is a mix of American and Southwestern, and they serve up some good margaritas.

HOUSE ON THE ROCK RESORT

400 Springs Drive
Spring Green, WI 53588
608-588-7000
www.thehouseontherock.com

COST: $145 and up.

CREDIT CARDS: American Express, Visa, Master-Card, Discover.

DESCRIPTION: More Frank Lloyd Wright than House on the Rock, this small resort boasts an indoor pool and a golf course, and it's just down the road from the American Players Theater, one of the best places in the country to catch Shakespeare outdoors.

TALIESIN

5607 County Road C
Spring Green, WI 53588
608-588-7900
www.taliesinpreservation.org

DESCRIPTION: Frank Lloyd Wright lived and worked here, and there are plenty of tours to be had. The best is the all-day, all-inclusive tour, which even features a snack on Frank's patio (but don't call him Frank—he's Mr. Wright).

HOUSE ON THE ROCK

5754 Highway 23
Spring Green, WI 53588
608-935-3639
www.thehouseontherock.com

DESCRIPTION: The House on the Rock is design on steroids . . . it is one man's vision of design, and inside, it sports collections of almost everything imaginable, from ships to bicycles to player musical instruments (for a quarter, you can hear and watch them play). It is goofy, but it's also a lot of fun for kids. It's sort of the anti–Frank Lloyd Wright.

AMERICAN PLAYERS THEATER

P.O. Box 819
Spring Green, WI 53588
608-588-2361
www.playinthewoods.org

DESCRIPTION: This is one of the best places to catch Shakespeare and classical theater outside. Some of the country's best Shakespeare an actors head to Spring Green for the summer and fall . . . and if it rains, the show still goes on.

MONROE/GREEN COUNTY

Green County has the largest concentration of master cheesemakers in the state, and it's a perfect jumping-off point for visiting cheese-makers in Green County and beyond.

CHALET LANDHAUS INN

801 Highway 69
New Glarus, WI 53574
608-527-5234

COST: Rates start at $69.

CREDIT CARDS: MasterCard, Visa, Discover, American Express.

DESCRIPTION: This little hotel, which boasts a really nice indoor pool and fitness center, offers Swiss-styled accommodations, with breakfast included.

INN SERENDIPITY

7843 County P
Browntown, WI 53522
608-329-7056
www.innserendipity.com

COST: Rates start at $105.

DESCRIPTION: This environmentally conscious bed & breakfast uses a wind turbine and solar panels for power. Only two guest rooms.

BAUMGARTNER'S CHEESE STORE AND TAVERN

1023 16th Avenue
Monroe, WI 53566
608-325-6157

COST: Inexpensive.

DESCRIPTION: This gem in downtown Monroe has one of the best cheese cases around, as well as an inviting, rustic wood bar and Swiss décor. The signature sandwich is Limburger and liver sausage on rye, but save room for home-made soups and desserts.

THE RATSKELLER AT TURNER HALL

1217 17th Avenue
Monroe, WI 53566
608-325-3461

COST: Midpriced.

DESCRIPTION: There are plenty of German ratskellers or beer halls around, but Monroe's ratskeller is the only Swiss one. Swiss food and Swiss heritage abounds, as every first Tuesday a local Swiss society meets to enjoy Swiss dining and culture.

HISTORIC CHEESEMAKING CENTER

(ALSO GREEN COUNTY WELCOME CENTER)
2108 Seventh Avenue
Monroe, WI 53566
608-325-4636

DESCRIPTION: Housed in an old railroad depot where barrels of Swiss used to be shipped out, is a caseophile's find, as this little center is packed to the brim with Wisconsin cheese history, including even an old phone booth where cheese buyers used to call in sales at the old Cheese Exchange in Green Bay.

NEW GLARUS BREWING COMPANY

County Trunk W and Highway 69
New Glarus, WI 53574
608-27-5850
www.newglarusbrewing.com

DESCRIPTION: One of Wisconsin's best small breweries. Come in and take a self-guided audio tour, and then sample some of their brews; especially try their Spotted Cow.

EAU CLAIRE/CHIPPEWA VALLEY/TWIN CITIES

Less than an hour from the Twin Cities, the Eau Claire/Chippewa Valley area is a great jumping-off point for several northwestern Wisconsin cheesemakers. Plus, it's just a cool little area.

The Twin Cities are an amazing metropolitan area, an area that basically extends to the border with Wisconsin, making it a great starting point for visiting Northwest Wisconsin creameries.

THE WILDWOOD LODGE

8511 Hudson Boulevard
Lake Elmo, MN 55042
866-294-6250
www.thewildwoodlodge.com

COST: $189–509.

CREDIT CARDS: Visa, MasterCard, Discover, American Express.

DESCRIPTION: Plush and luxurious without being over the top, The Wildwood Lodge boasts well-appointed rooms and an indoor pool and fitness center, and it is attached to the Machine Shed restaurant, where you get breakfast vouchers. It's also just across the Mississippi from Wisconsin and less than 30 minutes from Bass Lake Cheese Factory.

AMERICINN MOTEL & SUITES

11 W. South Avenue
Chippewa Falls, WI 54729
715-723-5711
www.americinn.com

COST: $85–$145, summer; $80–145, winter.

CREDIT CARDS: Visa, MasterCard, Discover, American Express.

DESCRIPTION: This little motel boasts an indoor pool with a slide, and a full breakfast buffet. The rooms are comfortable, some with whirlpools.

JACOB LEINENKUGEL BREWING COMPANY

124 E. Elm Street
Chippewa Falls, WI 54729
715-723-5557
www.leinie.com

DESCRIPTION: What's beer without cheese? Leinie's is the seventh oldest operating brewery in the country, and it's got a great tour.

OLSON'S ICE CREAM PARLOR & DELI

611 N. Bridge Street
Chippewa Falls, WI 54729
715-723-4331

COST: Reasonable.

DESCRIPTION: Olson's has been making "Homaid" ice cream since 1923, and they offer 20 different flavors to choose from. A cute little place to catch a quick bite to eat.

SHEBOYGAN AREA

Sheboygan is a good jumping-off point for cheesemakers in northeastern Wisconsin, and there's plenty to do, especially in Kohler.

THE AMERICAN CLUB

444 Highland Drive
Kohler, WI 53044
800-344-2838, ext. 700

COST: $300 and up, summer; $235 and up, winter.

CREDIT CARDS: MasterCard, Visa, American Express, Discover.

DESCRIPTION: As the Midwest's only AAA Five Diamond Resort, this is more than plush, offering some of the best golfing, dining, and spa experiences around. The American Club also features one of the best wine and cheese bars in the country, and it specializes in Wisconsin cheese. Every fall, they also host a huge Food and Wine Experience, bringing in famed winemakers and chefs from around the country.

THE OSTHOFF RESORT

101 Osthoff Avenue
Elkhart Lake, WI 53020-0151
800-876-3399
www.osthoff.com

COST: $225 and up, summer; $185 and up, winter.

CREDIT CARDS: MasterCard, Visa, American Express, Discover.

DESCRIPTION: Right on the banks of Elkhart Lake, a freshwater lake, this charming and luxurious resort boasts a new spa, as well as boating, biking, and plenty of other activities. But one of the big draws is its new cooking school, run by chef Jill Prescott, of PBS fame. To find out more about the school, visit www.jill prescott.com.

JOHN MICHAEL KOHLER ARTS CENTER

608 New York Avenue
Sheboygan, WI 53081
920-458-6144
www.jmkac.org

DESCRIPTION: This visual and performing arts center houses the world's largest collection of environment builders, self-taught or outside artists who turned their entire homes or estates

The American Club is one of the plushest resorts in the country.

into works of art. Also, as each public restroom was designed by an artist, its restrooms are among the most beautiful and extravagant in the world.

BAYFIELD

To visit the Tetzner Dairy, you need to drive up to one of the northernmost points in Wisconsin. Fortunately, the area is also one of the most incredibly beautiful regions in the state, as the North Woods and Lake Superior offer some of the most breathtaking scenery anywhere. Bayfield also features some of the best apple orchards in the Midwest.

ARTESIAN HOUSE
BED AND BREAKFAST

84100 Hatchery Road
Bayfield, WI 54814
715-779-3338
www.artesianhouse.com

COST: $115 and up, summer; $100 and up, winter.

CREDIT CARDS: Not accepted; pay cash or check.

DESCRIPTION: Four plush, private rooms with baths, and each one has access to the private deck. One of the best places to enjoy the North Woods, with gorgeous views of trees, flowers, and nature. The inn is eco-friendly, and host Al Chechik makes magnificent breakfasts from scratch each morning.

Relax on this wrap-around porch at the Artesian House.

WILD RICE RESTAURANT

84860 Old San Road
Bayfield, WI 54814
715-779-9881
www.wildricerestaurant.com

COST: Expensive.

DESCRIPTION: This isn't your typical "up north" restaurant. Instead, it's wildly inventive, with an extensive wine (and pretty extensive cheese) list and amazing food. The architecture is sublime, bringing the woods inside while showcasing the food, and the art is also pretty wild (especially the life-sized sculptured dolls in the women's restroom). Not open in winter months, though.

157

BLUE VISTA FARM

County Highway J and Hatchery Road
Bayfield, WI 54814
715-779-5400
www.bluevistafarm.com

DESCRIPTION: This environmentally friendly farm not only has organic berries and eco-friendly apples, but it also boasts some gorgeous flower gardens that attract hummingbirds. They also host some wine and cheese evenings featuring artisanal Wisconsin cheeses.

SUPERIOR VIEW FARM

86565 County Highway J
Bayfield, WI 54814
715-779-5404
www.superiorviewfarm.com

DESCRIPTION: This farm boasts one of the best views of Lake Superior around, but it also features a great little winery, too.

ERICKSON'S ORCHARD

86600 Betzold Road
Bayfield, WI 54814
715-779-5438
www.ericksonsorchard.com

DESCRIPTION: They make all their own jams, preserves, and baked goods, including some incredibly delicious apple donuts, right in the farm store.

APOSTLE ISLANDS CRUISE SERVICE

City Dock
Bayfield, WI 54814
715-779-3925
www.apostleisland.com

DESCRIPTION: You can't go to Bayfield without experiencing Lake Superior, and one of the best ways to enjoy it is to take a cruise around the Apostle Islands. These narrated cruises sometimes also include stopovers at the lighthouses on the islands.

BAYFIELD HERITAGE TOURS

P.O. Box 986
Bayfield, WI 54814
715-779-0299
http://bayfieldheritagetours.com

DESCRIPTION: This little tour company offers some of the best walking tours in the Midwest, combining history with entertainment. Especially recommended is the night ghost tour; although you carry candle lanterns, it's more friendly than spooky.

DAY TRIPS TO CHEESEMAKERS

*T*F YOU ARE PLANNING TO VISIT WISCONSIN'S CHEESEMAKERS AND dairy artisans, you probably should plan on spending anywhere from one to three hours per cheesemaker, and ideally, you probably can visit three in one day, including driving. And, yes, you will be doing a lot of driving if you visit Wisconsin's cheesemakers.

Here are some suggested groupings for visits:

If you are using Milwaukee as a base, Widmer's and Crave Brothers are both within an hour of the city limits. However, it would be challenging to visit both in the same day, as Widmer's is north and Crave Brothers is west. But you could include Widmer's on your way to visit Caprine Supreme.

Caprine Supreme could also be the end destination if you visit Henning's and Saxon Creamery, using Sheboygan as a base.

If you plan on visiting northwest Wisconsin, then Bass Lake, Crystal Ball, Blaser's, and LoveTree are all within relatively easy drives from each other. If Blaser's is your last stop, then you could easily visit Davis Farm, and from there, you could head up to see Tetzner's Dairy and beautiful Lake Superior.

If you head south, however, you could hit Castle Rock, Weber, and Hollands—all within an easy drive from each other.

Southwest Wisconsin creameries are sometimes close together, and sometimes a bit far apart. Mt. Sterling, Sibby's, Hidden Springs, and K & K/Natural Valley are all within easy driving distance from each other. Carr Valley is also near both K & K, and Cedar Grove.

Blue Marble and Dreamfarm are an easy drive from each other, as are Hook's, Brunkow, and Montforte. The easiest day trip of all, however, is in Green County. Roth Käse, Edelweiss, and Chalet are all within 20 minutes of each other.

MAP OF CHEESEMAKERS

1. Southwestern Wisconsin

1. K & K Cheese / Natural Valley Cheeses and Pasture Pride Cheeses
2. Hidden Springs Creamery
3. Sibby's Organic Ice Cream
4. Mount Sterling Cheese Cooperative
5. Montforte-Wisconsin Farmer's Union Specialty Cheese Company
6. Hook's Cheese Company
7. Brunkow Cheese
8. Edelweiss Town Hall Creamery
9. Roth Käse
10. Chalet Cheese Cooperative
11. Uplands Cheese Company
12. Capri Cheesery
13. Montchevré-Betin

2. South Central Wisconsin

1. Carr Valley Cheese
2. Cedar Grove Cheese / Wisconsin Sheep Dairy Cooperative
3. Dreamfarm
4. Blue Marble Dairy
5. Dane County Farmer's Market
6. Fantôme Farm
7. Crave Brothers Farmstead Cheese

3. Northwestern Wisconsin

1. Tetzner Dairy
2. LoveTree Farmstead Cheese
3. Blaser's USA Inc.
4. Crystal Ball Organic Farms
5. Bass Lake Cheese Factory
6. Castle Rock Organic Dairy
7. Weber Dairy
8. Holland's Family Cheese
9. Davis Farm

4. Eastern Wisconsin

1. Caprine Supreme
2. Saxon Creamery
3. Henning's Cheese
4. Widmer Cheese Cellars
5. BelGioioso Cheese
6. Sartori Foods

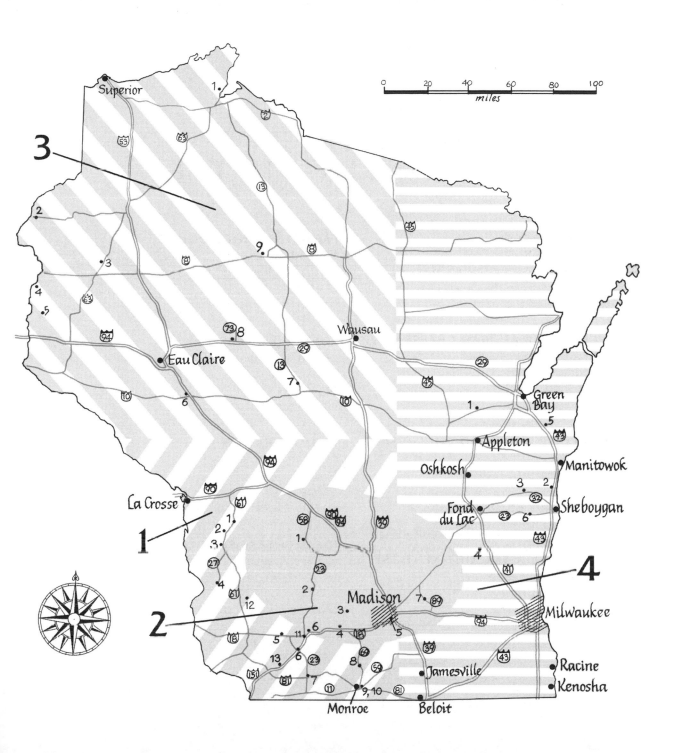

SHOPPING FOR WISCONSIN CHEESE

CENTRAL MARKET
4001 N. Lamar
Austin, TX 78756
512-206-1000
www.centralmarket.com

CHEESETIQUE ARTISAN CHEESE SHOP
2403 Mount Vernon Avenue
Alexandria, VA 22301
703-706-5300
www.cheesetique.com

COURTYARD WINE AND CHEESE BAR
66 Main Street
Rosemary Beach, FL 32461
850-231-1219
www.rosemarybeach.com/rosemary_beach_
dining.aspx

ENO (HOTEL INTERCONTINENTALS)
505 N. Michigan Avenue
Chicago, IL 60611
312-944-4100
www.enowinerooms.com

FARMSTEAD CHEESE SHOP
186 Wayland Avenue
Providence, RI 02906
401-274-7177
www.farmsteadinc.com

FOSTER & DOBBS
2518 NE 15th Avenue
Portland, OR 97212
503-284-1157
http://fosteranddobbs.com

FROMAGINATION
12 S. Carroll Street
Madison, WI 53703
608-255-2430
www.fromagination.com

IDEAL CHEESE SHOP
942 First Avenue
New York, NY 10022
800-382-0109
www.idealcheese.com

LARRY'S MARKET
8737 N. Deerwood Drive
Brown Deer, WI 53209
414-355-9650
www.larrysmarket.com

MARION STREET CHEESE MARKET
101 N. Marion Street
Oak Park, IL 60301
708-848-2088
www.marionstreetcheesemarket.com

MURRAY'S CHEESE
254 Bleecker Street
New York, NY 10014
212-243-3289
www.murrayscheese.com

NALA'S FROMAGERIE
2633 Development Drive
Green Bay, WI 54311
920-347-0334
www.nalascheese.com

PASTORAL ARTISAN CHEESE STORE
2945 N. Broadway Street
Chicago, Il 60657
773-472-4781
www.pastoralartisan.com

PREMIER CHEESE MARKET
5013 France Avenue S.
Minneapolis, MN 55410
612-436-5590

SAXELBY CHEESEMONGERS
Essex Street Market
New York, NY 10002
212-228-8204
www.saxelbycheese.com

SENDIK'S BROOKFIELD
18985 W. Capitol Drive
Brookfield, WI 53045
262-781-8200
www.sendiks.cc

VINTNER GRILL
10100 W. Charleston Boulevard, Suite 150
Las Vegas, NV 89135
702-214-5590
www.vglasvegas.com

WEST ALLIS CHEESE & SAUSAGE SHOPPE
Milwaukee Public Market
400 N. Water Street
Milwaukee WI, 53202
414-289-8333
www.wacheese-gifts.com/default.asp

ZINGERMAN'S
2501 Jackson Avenue
Ann Arbor, MI 48103
888-636-8162
www.zingermans.com

RESOURCES FOR
BUDDING CHEESEMAKERS

AMERICAN CHEESE SOCIETY
304 W. Liberty Street, Suite 201
Louisville, KY 40202
502-583-3783
www.cheesesociety.org

**DAIRY BUSINESS
INNOVATION CENTER**
P.O. Box 14
Delavan, WI 53115
888-623-2269
www.dbicusa.org

**NEW ENGLAND CHEESE MAKING
SUPPLY**
P.O. Box 85
Ashfield, MA 01330
413-628-3808
www.cheesemaking.com

WISCONSIN MILK MARKETING BOARD
8418 Excelsior Drive
Madison, WI 53717
608-836-8820
www.wisdairy.com

© 2007 WISCONSIN MILK MARKETING BOARD, INC.

*Les Frères comes in two different sizes of wheels,
with Le Petit Frère (the "Little Brother") being the
small size.*

WINE, BEER, AND OTHER BEVERAGE PAIRINGS WITH WISCONSIN CHEESE

C HEESE AND WINE GO TOGETHER EVEN WHEN PAIRED ALMOST haphazardly. The same goes for cheese and beer, and some people even believe that beer tastes better with cheese than wine does (but there are also plenty of vinophiles who would argue otherwise).

What wine and beer do is cleanse your palate of the cheese, says Jaclyn Stuart, sommelier at the American Club in Kohler, Wisconsin. The effervescence of a champagne or a beer, especially, will remove the cloying, buttery cheese taste from your mouth.

Cheese will also, conversely, cleanse your palate from the wine or beer, removing the tannins and other flavors from your tongue, says Mary Falk, of LoveTree Farmstead Cheese. "What that means if you are eating cheese and drinking wine together is that every sip of wine will taste like that first sip, and every bite of cheese will taste like that first taste," Falk says. "An excellent pairing of wine and cheese makes the wine taste better than it would alone and it makes the cheese taste better than it would alone, and when you have that perfect pairing, it's just heaven."

Red wine tends to go better with stronger cheeses.

And though Wisconsin cheese goes with wines and beers from all over the globe, there are some great Wisconsin wines, definite beers, and even spirits that tango nicely with Wisconsin cheese.

Though there are more than 30 wineries in the state—all of them small and most of them very good (visit www.wiswine.com for more information)—one of my favorite Wisconsin winemakers is Stone's Throw, of Door County. In particular, I recommend Stone's Throw's Riesling and zinfandel. I've also had success in pairing their field-blend red and field-blend white wines. Of all their wines, however, their Riesling probably pairs well with a larger variety of cheeses.

Riesling, as Steve Ehlers, of Larry's Market in Milwaukee, says, is one of the best wines to pair with cheese. White wines, as a rule, pair better with cheese than red wines do because the tannins in some red wines can sometimes clash with cheese. Big reds like cabernet sauvignons often do not pair as well with cheeses. They'll taste all right, but they really won't bring out the best in most cheeses, and most cheeses will not bring out the best in those wines. It's also worth noting that heavily oaked chardonnays will also not always pair well with cheeses.

Pinot noir, however, is a very cheese-friendly red wine. The Wollersheim Winery in Wisconsin makes a particularly good reserve pinot noir. I've tasted this wine and found that it pairs well with a variety of Wisconsin cheeses.

White Winter Winery makes some great meads, which pair well with some of the stronger Wisconsin cheeses like Trade Lake Cedar.

Champagnes and sparkling wines go really well with cheeses, but I personally do not know of a good sparkling Wisconsin wine. Having said that, I'm sure someone will soon correct me. But since I do not at this time have a sparkling wine recommendation, I'd suggest any good brut champagne or sparkling wine to pair with almost any cheese.

Door Peninsula Winery makes a lot of different wines, but one sweet dessert wine that contrasts well with cheese is the Muscat Alexandria. The winery has a great wine restaurant, the Vineyard.

Fruit like apples can tie the flavors of cheese and wine together.

Though Wisconsin has dozens of wineries, it has more than 70 different breweries and brewpubs that brew their own beers, and just about all of them are excellent. Being a Milwaukee gal, I tend to root for the hometown teams, and in terms of breweries, my local favorites are Lakefront and Sprecher. But I also love New Glarus and Capital Brewing, and as far as widely distributed Wisconsin beers go, Leinenkugel's is probably my favorite.

As lighter wines tend to go better with cheeses, so do lighter beers. But some dark bocks really can stand up to strongly flavored cheeses. Again, it's the complement/contrast theory in practice. For some great specific beer-cheese pairing suggestions, I recommend visiting the Web site of Lucy Saunders, a Wisconsin author and beer expert, at www.beer cook.com. A very versatile beer for cheese is a red lager, but Saunders says she prefers to match up her cheeses with specific brews.

Spirits can also pair well with cheeses, and Wisconsin has two artisanal vodka makers that I'd recommend: Death's Door Vodka and Rehorst Vodka. Vodka, as a general rule, pairs well with tangy cheeses like blues and fresh chèvres (think blue cheese–stuffed olives and martinis, for example). Death's Door is made by chef and hotelier Leah Caplan, of Washington Hotel in Door County, and Rehorst is made by Guy Rehorst in Milwaukee.

Although I love endorsing Wisconsin-made beers, wines, and vodkas, I realize that if you do not live in the state, some of these artisan-made brews might not be readily available. What I would suggest, if you are setting up a wine and cheese pairing, is to do a dry run. Besides Riesling, pinot noir, and sparkling wines, other wines that often match up well with cheese include sangiovese, gewürztraminer, sauvignon blanc, and red zinfandel. Port and dessert wines like muscat also tend to go very well with strong or blue cheeses.

Buy several cheeses and several wines, then mix and match and taste them, seeing what works and what doesn't work. "It's not an exact science," says Julie Erickson, of Bass Lake Cheese Factory. "Every wine and every artisanal cheese is different, and everyone's tastes are also personal."

And Erickson should know, since she and her husband host wine tastings with their cheeses every Saturday at their creamery.

APPENDIX 6
CHEESE FLIGHTS AND TASTING PLATES

ASTING CHEESE IS THE BEST PART, AND THERE ARE SO MANY wonderful Wisconsin cheeses to enjoy. When I set up a flight, or tasting plate of cheeses, for friends or family members, there are two basic techniques I employ: horizontal or vertical tastings.

A horizontal tasting is the more traditional sort of cheese tasting. It's basically a variety of cheeses of different tastes, textures, and types. A typical horizontal tasting will include a variety of cheesemakers, milks, and colors. Usually I will select between three and eight different cheeses, and I serve them mild to strong, with blue always served last. Most experts don't recommend more than four to six, but if you are serving small portions, I've enjoyed as many as eight, for example, at the Wild Rice Restaurant in Bayfield, Wisconsin.

Here is one example of a Wisconsin horizontal tasting: Driftless lavender and honey, Carr Valley's Crema Kase, Marieke's Raw Milk Gouda, Les Frères, Pleasant Ridge Reserve, Trade Lake Cedar, an aged cheddar (Hook's or Widmer's seven year old cheddar), and a blue (Montforte's blue, Roth Käse's Buttermilk Blue, or Castlerock's blue).

KOHLER CO.

Nuts and fruit add flavor, color and texture to a cheese plate.

A vertical tasting, however, is when you take a single cheese and either serve a variety of the same cheese made by different cheesemakers, or the same type but of different ages made by the same cheesemaker. For example, set up a Wisconsin chèvre tasting—include fresh chèvres made by Bass Lake, Fantôme Farm, Dreamfarm, and Montchevré. Or include a variety of goat's milk cheeses—Mt. Sterling's Monterey Jack, Bass Lake's truffle goat, and Carr Valley's Cocoa Cardona. Or set up a straight blue tasting of different blues—Hook's four blues, Montforte's two blues, Castlerock's blue, and Roth Käse's blue.

Or, set up a tasting of the same cheese, but at different ages. At the American Club in Kohler, Wisconsin, for example, they have a vertical tasting of Hook's cheddar, starting with the fresh cheddar curds and going up to a 12-year-old cheddar.

Just as there are two basic ways to set up a tasting, there are two basic ways to serve tastings. The first, and probably easiest way, is to arrange the tasting on one or two platters, and have your guests serve themselves. The second is to serve small portions of each cheese on plates for all of your guests. A good rule of thumb is to serve about 2 to 4 ounces of cheese per guest, and buy the cheese the day of or the day before you are planning on serving it.

Fondue is another great way to enjoy cheese.

Let the cheese warm up to room temperature before you serve it, and when you plate the cheese, always keep the washed rinds and blues either on a separate plate or distinctly separated on the plates from the other cheeses. Also, if you are putting out a single platter of cheese, make sure you have an individual knife for each cheese.

Be sure to serve the cheese with crusty baguettes and crackers, along with some dried or fresh fruits and nuts. In general, plain and unflavored breads work best, but fruit and nut breads also complement cheese. Fresh berries, dried cranberries, cherries, apricots, fresh or dried figs, and sliced apples work well, as do almonds, hazelnuts, walnuts, and pecans, spiced or just lightly toasted. For Wisconsin-only tastings, I especially love using Wisconsin products like cranberries, cherries, and apples.

Jams, marmalades, and honey can also be drizzled over the cheese or placed out for your guests to dab on their cheeses. Port wine and balsamic vinegar can be good, too, and port is especially good for blue cheeses. Honey mustard can also be good, especially if you are serving Limburger (a classic way to serve Limburger is to pair it with a slice of red onion, a dab of honey mustard, a piece of liver sausage, and dark pumpernickel bread).

When I am setting up a cheese plate for a party, I usually like to go to one of my favorite local stores and taste the cheese before I purchase it. A good cheese merchant or maître fromager at a quality restaurant can introduce you to new finds or discover new ways of pairing old favorites. If you have a good cheese store in your area that sells Wisconsin cheeses, get to know the staff there. If Wisconsin cheeses, or the specific Wisconsin cheeses, aren't sold within your area, most cheesemakers either sell them direct on the Internet or over the phone, and there are some great stores that will also ship them to you.

It is best to eat your good cheeses within the week that you purchase them. Store them in your vegetable drawer (free of vegetables, of course), and if you need to wrap them up again after eating, use clean (not used) plastic, foil, or wax paper, or store them in a nice plastic or glass container.

I've also seen it suggested that you rub (except for blue cheeses) the cheeses with extra virgin olive oil before you wrap them up to better preserve them, but I haven't personally tried that (cheese generally does not last long in my house). Many experts say wax paper works best, but the main rule is to not overbuy and then have the cheese go bad in your refrigerator. Also, never store washed rinds or blues in the same container. Limburger always gets its own special glass container in my house. And if you have a bunch of different cheeses left over, try making homemade cheese spread (there's a recipe for that in the recipe section).

RECIPES FOR WISCONSIN CHEESE AND SUGGESTIONS FOR COOKING WITH CHEESE

I LOVE TO EAT CHEESE, BUT I ALSO ADORE COOKING WITH CHEESE. I have found that many dishes can be improved with a little addition of cheese.

When baking bread, I often will sprinkle a half cup or more either into the dough or on top of the crust. Most of the salads I make have fresh chèvre, crumbled blue cheese, or Parmesan sprinkles. And even when I make dog treats, I often add cheese.

When you cook with real cheese, the main thing you need to know is that it doesn't behave anything like processed cheese. Remember that if you heat up cheese too high, the casein or protein in the cheese will separate from the fat, and that can sometimes turn into a big mess. Use medium or medium low heat and be gentle with your cheese. Starch, wine, and lemon juice can also be used to prevent cheese from becoming gloppy if you cook it—that's easily shown in any fondue recipe, which usually calls for one or all three ingredients.

Cheese also melts better if it is shredded or grated, and cheese shreds more easily if it is cold. In all other cases you would want to warm your cheese up to room temperature, but not if you are grating.

Lastly, experiment with using different cheeses in your recipes, and combining cheeses is also fun. Whenever I make macaroni and cheese or just a grilled cheese sandwich, I often use two or more cheeses. But I always keep in mind that when I use Wisconsin artisanal cheeses, they often have intense flavors, so a little can go a long way. If you're using a high-quality blue cheese, say Hook's Tilston Point, you don't need a lot of it to flavor your salad.

APPETIZERS

VINTNER GRILL SEASONAL JAM
(FOR SERVING WITH CHEESE)
FROM CHEF MATTHEW SILVERMAN OF VINTNER GRILL, LAS VEGAS

- 4 cups water
- 3 pounds fruit (seasonal and fresh, especially recommended are champagne grapes)
- 1.5 ounces pectin
- ½ cup sugar

Mix all ingredients in a medium saucepan over medium high heat. Bring to a boil. Taste for desired sweetness (if you prefer it sweeter, you will need to add more sugar). Cool and serve with cheese.

FETA AND TOMATO APPETIZER
INSPIRED BY CAPRI CHEESE'S FETA TOMATO SAUCE

- 8 ounces feta
- 2 cups diced fresh tomatoes
- ½ cup white wine
- 3 tablespoons fresh basil, minced
- 1 tablespoon extra virgin olive oil
- 1 teaspoon dried Italian seasoning
- 2 cloves garlic, minced
- salt, pepper to taste

Preheat oven to 350 degrees. In a medium-sized bowl, mix tomatoes, wine, olive oil, garlic, basil, Italian seasoning, salt, and pepper. In an ovenproof casserole dish, place feta. Pour tomato mixture around feta. Bake in oven for 20 to 30 minutes or until cheese is golden brown but not burned. Serve with toasted bread or crackers. *Makes 6 to 8 appetizer servings. For a variation, use chèvre or blue cheese.*

CARAMELIZED ONION, SPINACH, AND PARMESAN DIP

- 2 cups sour cream
- 1 large onion, diced
- 1 cup cooked spinach, frozen or fresh
- 1 cup shredded Stravecchio Parmesan or Grana Americano
- 2 cloves garlic, minced
- 2 tablespoons olive oil or butter
- 2 teaspoons Cajun seasoning
- salt, pepper to taste

Heat a large saucepan over high heat. Add the oil, heat for 10 seconds, and then add the onions. Sauté until caramelized. Set aside and let cool. Mix rest of ingredients in a large bowl. Add the onions. Serve. Can also heat in a casserole and then serve warm, too. *Makes about 3½–4 cups dip.*

HEARTH BREAD

FROM SARAH DOWHOWER, MY STEPMOTHER-IN-LAW

- 1 pound Emmentaler or Baby Swiss cheese, sliced thinly
- 1 pound or package of good bacon
- 1 loaf crusty Italian bread
- 1 stick of butter, unsalted and softened
- 1½ tablespoons Dijon mustard
- ⅓ cup diced white onion
- 1 tablespoon poppy seeds
- 3 dashes of hot sauce
- salt, pepper to taste

Preheat oven to 350 degrees. In a large bowl, mix everything except the cheese and the bread. Slice the bread almost all the way through but not quite. Put about 1 teaspoon or more of the mixture between the slices. Then, put the slices of cheese in between the slices. Pack bread loaf back together, laying strips of bacon over the top. Wrap in foil, but leave the top open. Bake for 20 to 30 minutes or until the bacon is golden brown. *Makes about 8 to 10 appetizer servings.*

WISCONSIN RACLETTE CHEESE, DRIED FIG, AND TRUFFLE PASTY
FROM THE AMERICAN CLUB IN KOHLER

- 8 ounces dried figs, cut into quarters
- 3 ounces cider vinegar
- 3 ounces sugar
- 2 tablespoons white truffle oil
- 1 winter truffle, chopped
- 1 teaspoon salt
- 1 teaspoon black pepper
- 8 ounces Wisconsin Raclette cheese, cut into 16 equal pieces
- 14 ounces puff pastry dough, thawed and rolled into 16 thin squares
- 1 egg, beaten
- 2 egg yolks, beaten

Soak the figs in vinegar overnight. In a small pan over low heat, bring the figs, sugar, and vinegar to a gentle boil. Let boil for about 15 minutes, stirring occasionally. Pull the pan off the stove and add the truffle oil and truffle pieces, along with salt and pepper. Mix well and allow to cool down. Preheat oven to 400 degrees Fahrenheit. Place a piece of the Raclette cheese just off center on each puff pastry square. Spoon a teaspoon of the fig mixture on top. Moisten edges of pastry with egg wash. Fold each pastry in half to form a half moon shape. Crimp edges to seal. Brush each pasty with egg yolk and bake on a silicone-lined cookie sheet for 20 minutes or until golden and puffed. Spoon leftover fig and truffle mix on top and serve. *Makes 16 appetizers.*

FROMAGE FORT, OR HOMEMADE CHEESE SPREAD
WHAT TO DO WITH LEFTOVER CHEESE

- ⅓ pound leftover cheese
- 2 sticks of butter
- ½ cup white wine
- 3 big cloves of garlic
- ½ teaspoon sugar
- salt, white pepper to taste

Place all ingredients in a food processor. Chop until finely mixed. If it is not creamy enough, add a drizzle more of wine. *Makes about 2 cups cheese spread.*

SIDES AND SALADS

BLUE CHEESE POTATO SALAD

3 pounds small red potatoes, cut in half, boiled, and drained
1 cup crumbled blue cheese, plus ½ cup crumbled blue cheese reserved
   (like Hook's, Montforte, Castlerock, or Roth Käse's Buttermilk Blue)
½ cup mayonnaise
½ cup reduced-fat sour cream
½ cup celery, diced
½ cup red onion, diced
4 slices bacon, cooked to crisp and crumbled
2 teaspoons rice vinegar
½ teaspoon garlic powder
½ teaspoon Cajun seasoning
2 tablespoons chopped parsley or chives (optional)
   salt, pepper to taste

Boil potatoes, then drain and set aside. In a food processor, blend 1 cup of blue cheese with mayonnaise, sour cream, vinegar, and spices. Mix together potatoes, mayo/blue cheese mix, celery, onion, and bacon. Then mix reserved ½ cup of blue cheese. Add salt, pepper to taste. Sprinkle with chopped parsley or chives. Chill. *Makes 8 cups.*

BLUE CHEESE DRESSING

½ pound blue cheese
½ cup mayonnaise, preferably light
⅓ cup sour cream, preferably light
2 tablespoons rice wine vinegar
1 tablespoon extra virgin olive oil
1 teaspoon Cajun seasoning
½ teaspoon garlic salt
½ teaspoon Dijon mustard

Place all the ingredients in a food processor or blender. *Makes about 2 cups of blue cheese dressing.*

GOAT CHEESE AND STRAWBERRY SALAD

For the goat cheese crottins:

6 ounce log of chèvre, plain or with herbs
1 cup chopped nuts (pecans or walnuts)

For the salad:

6 cups mixed greens
1½ cups sliced fresh strawberries
½ cup red onion, thinly sliced with a mandolin
½ cup red pepper, thinly sliced

For the dressing:

¼ cup extra virgin olive oil
⅛ cup balsamic vinegar
1 tablespoon poppy seeds
2 teaspoons Dijon mustard
1 teaspoon extra fine or caster sugar
salt, pepper to taste

Slice chèvre log into six rounds (to keep from crushing, use an old, but clean, guitar string). Roll chèvre slices in nuts (you will not use all the nuts). Place rounds on a cookie sheet. Cover with plastic wrap and put in freezer for 20 minutes. Mix together salad greens, onions, peppers, and strawberries. Set aside. Whisk together ingredients for dressing. Toss salad with dressing and divide into six plates or bowls. Turn on broiler. Remove plastic wrap, place cookie sheet with goat cheese rounds in oven. Bake for about 4 to 5 minutes or until goat cheese is lightly browned and toasty, but not completely oozing or melting. Remove from oven, top salads with rounds, and serve. *Serves 6.*

OUTPOST NATURAL FOODS SIGNATURE SPINACH AND CHICKPEA SALAD
FROM OUTPOST NATURAL FOODS. MILWAUKEE

- 1 ounce baby spinach, chopped
- ½ pound feta cheese, cubed into quarter-inch pieces
- ½ pound red peppers, diced into quarter-inch pieces
- 30 ounces or two 15-ounce cans organic chickpeas, drained and rinsed
- 1 tablespoon lemon juice
- 1 teaspoon ground cumin
- ¾ teaspoon black pepper
- ½ teaspoon garlic, minced
- ⅛ cup extra virgin olive oil
- salt, pepper to taste

Combine spinach, feta, red peppers, and chickpeas in a large bowl. In a small bowl, combine lemon juice, cumin, pepper, and garlic. Slowly whisk in olive oil.

Pour dressing over chickpeas and toss well to combine. Season with salt and pepper to taste. Refrigerate for at least two hours before serving. *Serves 8.*

YUKON GOLD GOAT CHEESE GRATIN
FROM CHEF DAN SMITH FROM McCORMICK & SCHMICK'S SEAFOOD RESTAURANT

- 2 pounds large Yukon gold potatoes (4–5), peeled and sliced ⅛ inch to ¼ inch
- 1 cup heavy cream
- ½ cup crumbled Montchevré chèvre or Fantôme Farm chèvre
- ½ cup grated Sarvecchio, aged Asiago, or Belgioioso American Grana
  freshly ground black pepper and kosher salt to taste

Preheat oven to 350. Butter a 13 x 9 x 2-inch baking dish, or an 8-cup gratin dish. Arrange one layer of potatoes in dish and drizzle ¼ of the cream, sprinkle ¼ of the cheeses, grind a bit of black pepper, and add a pinch of salt to layer. Continue this process with each layer until all ingredients are used (reserve or add a little extra cheese and cream for top layer). Cover with aluminum foil. Bake 40–45 minutes. Remove foil and bake another 15 minutes or until top is golden brown and bubbly. This is a very versatile dish. Serve with braised beef short ribs, a simply roasted chicken, or grilled lamb chops. An excellent California pinot noir would pair perfectly. *Makes 8 servings.*

ENTREES

SANTA FE CHICKEN QUESADILLA
FROM BUFFALO PHIL'S GRILLE, WISCONSIN DELLS

- 1 **pound of diced, precooked chicken**
- 2 **cups shredded cheese (Monterey Jack and cheddar suggested)**
- 1 **cup Hellman's Ancho Chipotle Sandwich Sauce**
- 1 **cup thick and chunky salsa**
- 2 **teaspoons Cajun seasoning**
- 8 **flour tortillas, 7-inch**
- ¼ **cup melted butter**

Mix shredded cheeses with Cajun seasoning and set aside. Brush two tortillas with butter. Lay one tortilla buttered side down. Spread tortilla with 2 tablespoons of ancho chipotle sauce and layer with 4 ounces of chicken and ¼ cup of the cheese mixture. Top with second tortilla buttered side up. Place layered tortillas buttered side down in a large fry pan or in a George Forman type grill. Grill for one to three minutes in pan, then turn over and grill an additional one to three minutes. If using a grill, simply close the cover and grill one to three minutes. Repeat process with remaining tortillas and ingredients. Remove, slice into wedges, and arrange on plate. Serve with ¼ cup salsa. *Makes 4 servings as an appetizer or 2 servings as a meal.*

CHÈVRE CHEESE STUFFED CHICKEN SICILIAN STYLE
FROM CHEF MICHAEL FEKER, IL MITO RESTAURANT, MILWAUKEE

For the chicken breasts:
- 4 boneless chicken breasts (7 ounces each), butterflied and pounded
- 12 ounces sautéed spinach
- 1 red pepper, roasted, peeled, and quartered
- 12 ounces fresh chèvre
- 8 ounces Parmesan
- 4 teaspoons Italian parsley, chopped
- ¾ cup of flour (6 ounces)
- 2 eggs
- ½ cup milk
- salt, pepper to taste

Bread crumb mixture:
- 1 cup plain bread crumbs
- 4 ounces Romano
- 1 ounce dry thyme, crumbled fine
- 2 teaspoons granulated garlic
- salt, pepper to taste

- 6 ounces extra virgin olive oil

Preheat oven to 350 degrees Fahrenheit. Pound and butterfly chicken and season each breast with salt and pepper. Top chicken with spinach, red pepper, chèvre, Parmesan and parsley. Fold chicken with ingredients inside. Lightly dust each piece of chicken with flour. Whisk eggs and milk in bowl. Combine ingredients for bread crumb mixture. First roll chicken in milk-egg mix, then roll into the bread crumb mixture, covering well. Heat skillet to low-medium and add olive oil. Lightly sauté the chicken until golden brown on both sides. Bake for 12 to 15 minutes or until done. Serve with some buttered pasta and fresh lemon. *Makes 4 servings.*

BASIC SWISS FONDUE

LARRY'S MARKET, MILWAUKEE

- 6 ounces Emmentaler, grated
- 6 ounces Gruyère, grated
- 4 ounces another cheese (Appenzeller, Fontina, or Gouda, for example), grated
- 1 clove garlic
- 1½ cups dry, white wine
- 1 tablespoon lemon juice
- 1 rounded teaspoon flour
  - pepper, nutmeg to taste
- 2 loaves of crusty Italian or French bread, cubed or cut in slices with a bit of crust on each piece

Dredge cheese with flour. Rub inside of pot with cut garlic clove. Place pot on stove. Pour wine into pot. Heat over medium flame until wine is hot, but not boiling. Add lemon juice. Add handfuls of cheese, stirring constantly with wooden spoon until cheese is melted and the cheese-wine mixture has the appearance of a light, creamy sauce. Add pepper and nutmeg to taste. Bring to a boil, then remove pot and place on lighted burner on top of table. Adjust the flame of burner so fondue continues bubbling very lightly. Serve each guest a handful of bread cubes from a plate or basket. Spear fork through soft part of bread first, securing prongs in crust. Dunk to bottom of pot and stir well. Remove fork and twist over pot. *Makes 2 to 4 servings.*

Other fondue twists: For a beer and cheese fondue, use a couple of cheddars and/or jacks instead of Emmentaler/Gruyère, and substitute the wine with a lager or an ale, also adding 1 teaspoon of Dijon mustard.

Another great fondue is caramelized onions with Gouda: Use all Gouda, with perhaps a quarter cup of Baby Swiss, and add 1 cup of diced, caramelized onions. To caramelize onions: Heat a saucepan over high heat (until water dances on the pan), add 1 tablespoon of oil, heat for at least 10 seconds, then add onions. Sauté until caramelized. Set aside until ready to make fondue.

BEC'S MOM'S MAC 'N CHEESE

½ stick unsalted butter
1 medium onion, diced
2 tablespoons white flour
1 teaspoon dried oregano
2 cups macaroni
3½ cups milk
2 cups cheese, grated (recommended to use a mix of cheese like cheddar, Gouda, and Parmesan, etc.)
  salt, pepper to taste

In a large saucepan, sauté onion in butter over medium high heat until translucent. Add flour, oregano, salt, and pepper; stir until it becomes a paste. Add macaroni, then add milk, and make sure macaroni is completely covered in milk. Cook until macaroni is tender, about 20 minutes. Then stir in cheese and serve. *Makes 4 servings.*

SCRAMBLED EGGS WITH CHEESE AND TRUFFLE OIL

2 eggs
2 tablespoons butter
2 tablespoons cream
2 tablespoons grated cheese (truffle cheese or Parmesan)
1 tablespoon fresh chives, minced
  drizzle of black truffle oil
  salt, pepper to taste

Whisk together the eggs and cream. In a medium saucepan over medium heat, melt butter. Add eggs and stir until almost cooked. Add cheese and truffle oil. Sprinkle with chives and salt and pepper to taste and serve. *Makes 1 serving.*

SWEETS AND DESSERTS

GRUYÈRE AND APPLE TURNOVER, ROTH KÄSE

    sheet puff pastry
½ **cup Grand Cru Gruyère, shredded**
1 **apple, peeled, cored, and diced**
1 **teaspoon sugar**

Top pastry with cheese, sugar, and apples Fold into a "beggar's purse." Sprinkle a little extra sugar on top if desired. Bake at 350 degrees Fahrenheit for 25 minutes. *Makes 1 serving.*

CRAVE BROTHERS CHOCOLATE MASCARPONE PIE

Crust:
1 **cup chocolate wafer cookie crumbs**
¼ **cup butter, melted**
3 **tablespoons sugar**

Filling:
16 **ounces mascarpone (Crave Brothers Farmstead Classics)**
6 **ounces bittersweet or semisweet chocolate, melted**
2 **tablespoons Kahlúa or amaretto liqueur**

Preheat oven to 325 degrees Fahrenheit. Butter a 9-inch pie pan. Stir together the cookie crumbs, sugar, and melted butter. Press crumbs evenly in the pan. Bake for six minutes. Set aside to cool. In a large bowl, stir together the mascarpone and melted chocolate until blended with no white streaks. Stir in the liqueur. Immediately spread filling in the crust. Cover and refrigerate one hour. Top with whipped cream if desired. *Makes 8 servings.*

MASCARPONE OR VANILLA YOGURT FRUIT DIP
INSPIRED BY SARAH DOWHOWER'S RECIPE

1½ cups mascarpone or 1½ cups vanilla yogurt
½ cup superfine or caster sugar
½ cup Kahlúa or Bailey's Irish Cream
2 tablespoons ground bittersweet chocolate, plus 2 tablespoons reserved
1 tablespoon Tahitian vanilla

Mix together all ingredients except reserved chocolate. Chill for one hour. Sprinkle remaining chocolate on top and serve with strawberries, bananas, and pineapple chunks. *Makes about 2 cups dip.*

GRILLED PINEAPPLE AND JUUSTOLEIPA SKEWERS

For the skewers:
1 pound Juustoleipa, cut into cubes
1 pound fresh pineapple chunks

For the marinade:
½ cup dark rum
1 tablespoon extra virgin olive oil
1 tablespoon fresh lemon or lime juice
1 teaspoon Tahitian vanilla
1 teaspoon cinnamon
1 teaspoon fresh lemon or lime zest

Alternate pieces of Juusto with pineapple chunks. Mix rum and other marinade ingredients together. Brush skewers with rum mixture. Grill or broil each skewer about five minutes per side, then serve. *Makes about 4 servings.*

GLOSSARY

ACIDIFICATION: The process in which bacterial cultures affect and change the milk sugar or lactose into lactic acid during cheesemaking. The level of acidity affects the taste of the cheese.

AFFINAGE: This French word means the art of aging and refining cheese.

AFFINEUR/AFFINEUSE: A person who professionally ages or ripens cheese. In the American artisanal world, many of the cheesemakers are also the affineur or affineuse, but in some European countries, the cheeses are picked up from the cheesemaker and then aged by an affineur or affineuse.

AGED CHEESE: Cheese that has been ripened for several months or several years, depending on the cheese and the cheesemaker.

AGING CHEESE: To ripen cheese.

ANNATTO: This South American seed from the achiote tree gives cheddar its orange color.

AMERICAN ARTISAN: These are new, often original cheeses, crafted by American cheesemakers with care.

AROMA: The smell that comes from a cheese.

ARTISANAL: This is the opposite of industrial cheese. It is cheese that is handcrafted or crafted with care.

BLOOMY RIND: A cheese that has a soft, white rind like Brie.

BLUE CHEESE: Blue cheese has a mold added to create its distinctive blue or blue-green color and sharp flavors.

BOVINE GROWTH HORMONE: Bovine growth hormone, also known as somatotropin, is a hormone that is injected into cows to make them produce more milk (it is extracted from cows' pituitary glands). It is also known as recombinant bovine growth hormone or recombinant bovine somatotropin (rBGH or rBST). The recombinant version is a genetically engineered version that is most commonly used. Bovine growth hormone is allowed in the United States, but it is outlawed in Europe. Some studies suggest that it is hazardous to the health of humans, others say it is safe. Cows that have been injected with hormones typically have shorter milking lives than those who are milked naturally.

BRINE: A salt solution is used to make some firm and hard cheeses like Emmentaler or Gouda.

BROWSERS: Animals that eat leaves, bark, twigs, shrubs, and vines. Goats are browsers.

CASEIN: The milk protein in cheese takes its name from *caseus,* which is the Latin word for cheese.

CASEOPHILES: Caseophiles are people who love cheese.

CAVE: A cavern or hole dug into the earth for the purpose of aging cheese. Caves offer the right temperature and humidity for aging cheese.

CHEDDARING: The process of cutting, slabbing, and piling curds to press the whey out creates the cheese we call cheddar. This process was first created in England.

CHEESE CLOTH: A cotton cloth that is used to drain cheese curds.

CHEESE CONNOISSEURS: People who adore cheese. They are sometimes also called caseophiles or turophiles.

CHEESE COURSE: A separate course within a meal that is made up of just cheese, with perhaps some bread and fruit on the side. It is usually served sixth out of seven courses.

CHEESE HARP: A metal, harp-shaped paddle strung with linear blades. It is used by cheesemakers to cut curds in the cheese-making process.

CHÈVRE: In French, the word for goat is *chèvre*. This term also refers to the fresh cheese made from goat's milk.

COAGULATION: The process of when milk proteins stick together to form curds.

CREAM LINE: Milk that is not homogenized is known as cream line because there's a definitive line between the cream, which floats on top, and the milk, which is on the bottom.

CROTTIN: A small round of goat cheese, often coated with ash.

CULTURES: Bacteria are used to make cheese. These bacterial cultures break the milk down into curds and whey.

CURDS: The solid or coagulated portion of milk during cheesemaking are called curds, and they are the part that are aged to become cheese. In Wisconsin, they are often sold separately, and when they are really fresh, they squeak. They are not cheese leftovers or bits of cheese.

CUTTING THE CURDS: After the rennet has been introduced to the milk, curds are cut to expel additional whey.

EMMENTALER: This is what most people refer to as Swiss cheese. It was first made in the Alps of Switzerland, and Green County, Wisconsin, is where the bulk of American Emmentaler used to be made.

EWES: Female sheep.

FARMSTEAD CHEESE: Cheese made right on the same farm where the animals are raised and milked.

FERMENTATION: The process in which milk becomes cheese or yogurt. It is the breakdown of carbohydrates in a food, which changes the original substance into something new.

FETA: This Greek sheep's milk cheese is sometimes made in the United States from goat's milk or cow's milk; it is typically brined in salt.

FIRM: A cheese that has aged for a longer period of time than semisoft is considered firm. A firm cheese is harder to the touch than semisoft, but softer than hard cheese.

FREE-STALL: This type of barn, which doesn't have any individual stalls, allows the cows to roam freely within the barn.

FRESH: A cheese that has not been aged or ripened is called fresh—like mozzarella or chèvre.

GRAZERS: Animals that primarily eat grass and clover, like cows and sheep.

GRUYÈRE: A hard, Swiss, cow's milk cheese that traditionally was made in the Alps and is prized for its ability to melt (thus it is often used in fondues).

HARD: A cheese that is aged for a long period of time and has lost a lot of moisture is hard, and it is also hard to the touch.

HOMOGENIZED: When fats are broken down in milk so that they are evenly distributed throughout the milk, the milk is homogenized. Homogenization allows milk to have a longer shelf life, and in whole milk, the fat will not separate out and float to the top. Homogenized milk is not used in making cheese.

JUUSTOLEIPA: This Finnish bread cheese is quite sweet. In Finland it is made from reindeer's milk, but in Wisconsin it is made from cow's milk.

LACTIC ACID: When the bacteria eat the sugars in milk during cheesemaking, lactic acid is formed.

LACTOSE: The sugar in milk is called lactose. Bacteria eat the lactose during the formation of cheese.

MAÎTRE FROMAGER: In fancy restaurants, they often have a cheese expert who has studied cheese and will help you navigate a restaurant's cheese selection. They are like a sommelier for cheese.

MAMMOTH CHEESE: Giant wheels of cheese.

MICROBIAL RENNET: In the past, most cheeses used rennet, an enzyme from the lining of calves' stomachs, to coagulate cheese. But today this enzyme is produced by microbes or bacteria, and it is more common than regular rennet in cheesemaking.

PASTE: The interior part of a cheese.

PASTEURIZATION: Milk is heated up to high temperatures to kill germs or unwanted bacteria. There are three types of pasteurization: gentle pasteurization, in which it is heated to 145 degrees Fahrenheit for 30 minutes, then cooled; high temperature, short time pasteurization, or HTST, in which it is heated to 161 degrees Fahrenheit for 15 seconds, then cooled; and ultra-high temperature pasteurization, or UHT, in which milk is heated to 200 degrees Fahrenheit for about two seconds then cooled. UHT is known in most quality dairy circles as "sterilization" because it ruins the taste. UHT is used for a longer shelf life; UHT milk can actually sit on the shelf for six months or longer without refrigeration.

PLUG A CHEESE: When a judge or cheesemaker removes a sample from a wheel of cheese, they plug the cheese.

PROCESSED CHEESE: This isn't really cheese. It is a cheese product. The cheese is heat-treated and mixed with emulsifiers and other additives that keep it from breaking down when heated.

RAW MILK: Unpasteurized milk.

rBGH: Recombinant bovine growth hormone is a synthetically produced, genetically engineered version of the growth hormone that is injected into cows to make them produce more milk.

RENNET: The enzyme used to coagulate cheese is called rennet. It is also known as chymosin, and it used to exclusively come from the stomachs of calves, but today most rennet is produced by microbes in a laboratory.

RICOTTA: An Italian cheese that used to be made from the leftover whey from mozzarella production.

RIND: The outside surface or skin of a cheese. Some cheeses have rinds, others do not, and different rinds are developed through different methods of cheesemaking.

RIPENING: The process of aging a cheese until it is ready to be sold and eaten is called ripening or affinaging.

ROTATIONAL GRAZING: When cows or other grazing animals are moved from differ-ent pastures on a regular schedule. Rotational grazing prevents the pastures from being overgrazed. Farmer Bert Paris says it's like giving his cows a clean plate, and it is actually easier on the farmer, as well as easier on the land.

SALTING: Salting or adding salt to the cheese curds is always part of the cheese-making process. Sometimes the salt is rubbed, sometimes it is mixed in with the cheese, and sometimes, wheels of cheese are floated in a saltwater solution. The salt helps stop the bacterial cultures from changing the cheese too much.

SEMISOFT: A cheese that has been aged longer than fresh cheeses but still is pliable and has enough moisture in it.

TERROIR: This French word explains how geography and different environments have a very distinctive effect on food products, especially cheese and wine. Artisanal cheese producers often describe how their environment, or terroir, affects the taste of their cheese.

TOMME: A small, flat wheel is called a tomme or sometimes a tome.

TRIER: This tool slightly resembles an apple corer, and it is used by professional cheese judges and cheesemakers to remove samples from large wheels of cheese.

TUROPHILES: Cheese lovers.

UMAMI: Besides, sweet, salty, sour, and bitter, there is a "fifth" taste called umami. It is sort of like a mushroom taste, and many cheeses have an umami flavor.

UNHOMOGENIZED: Milk that hasn't been homogenized or had its fats broken down and evenly distributed. Unhomogenized milk is the type of milk used in cheesemaking.

VAT: Vats or cheese vats are the large, stainless steel tanks in which milk is cooked and transformed into cheese.

WASHED RIND: Cheese in which the rind is washed with brine, salt, beer, wine, or some other mixture to create flavors is called a washed rind cheese. Washed rind cheeses have very strong aromas, but their intense smells often belie mild tastes.

WHEY: When cheese is made, there is a liquid protein that is left over, and that is called whey. It's part of what Miss Muffet was eating, and it used to be considered waste. Today, however, many cheesemakers sell their whey, which then gets incorporated into protein bars and many other foods. In Wisconsin, farmers used to drop off their milk, and then pick up cans of whey to feed to their hogs. When cheesemaker Scott Erickson used to deliver whey to some farmers, the pigs got to know the sound of his truck, and they started squealing when they heard him coming since they liked the taste of whey so much.

INDEX